THE SON OF A MONSTER

Investigation into the brain
of serial killer Michel Fourniret

Oli Porri Santoro

THE SON OF A MONSTER
Investigation into the brain
of serial killer Michel Fourniret

Max Milo
ESSAIS-DOCUMENTS

Max Milo Editions, Paris, 2023
www.maxmilo.com
ISBN : 978 231501 136 0

To Francesco "*Cicciù*" Santoro,
Nunziata Carla,
and Kyann, *in memoriam*

DEDICATION

I dedicate this book to a dear friend who died at the age of twenty-four.

On May 28, 2011, Kyann took his own life under the inert gaze of his parents, whose antidepressants he had to make sure they took every day to the point of forgetting to live. How many times did he find them, in turn, lying on the floor of their shabby suburban apartment, after a drug overdose?

And what about him? With his oily jet hair, he looked like he had just come out of the swamp of melancholy.

Kyann has been a faithful support for me. Without her help, this book would not have been possible.

You put me to shame thinking about what happened there!
You have shamed me! The dead listen to you.
Do you think they listen to this?
I only ask for the silence that the dead call for.
Robert Badinter

The most important thing in life,
is not to waste his talent.
Calogero "*Chazz*" Palminteri

1.

AWAKENING

"For whoever wants to save his soul, will lose it."
Gospel according to Mark

May 28, 2013

This afternoon, I am at my grandmother Giuseppa's house. I come across a rerun of *Faites entrer l'accusé*, the program brilliantly presented by Christophe Hondelatte. I've just gobbled up a hill of spaghetti with a wine-red sandstone, raised like a snow-capped peak of parmesan.

Michel Fourniret, and Monique Olivier...," the presenter begins, "together they went hunting, as they used to say, hunting for young virgins.

Michel Fourniret, better known under the nickname of "the ogre of the Ardennes", was known to me only by vague hearsay, or by press clippings, served by a few flashes of the pen. The names of Monique Olivier and Michel Fourniret sounded like the archetype of absolute evil. For me, they were of the same ilk as Emile Louis, Marc Dutroux, and a whole host of other criminals guilty of the most shameful of crimes, pedophilia... I was completely wrong, because according to Christophe Hondelatte, "Michel Fourniret and Monique Olivier form the most incredible couple of serial killers in criminal history.

At the end of a trial that began on March 27, 2008, the Ardennes Assize Court sentenced Michel Fourniret to life imprisonment with a measure of incompressibility for the kidnapping, rape and murder of seven young girls between 1987 and 2003. Among them, Isabelle Laville in December 1987 in Auxerre in the Yonne, Fabienne Leroy in August 1988 near Mourmelon in the Marne, Jeanne-Marie Desramault in March 1989 near Charleville-Mézières, Élisabeth Brichet in December 1989 in Namur in Belgium, Natacha Danais, in November 1990 near Nantes, Céline Saison in May 2000 in Charleville-Mézières, and Mananya Thumpong in May 2001 in Sedan, in the Ardennes.

"The youngest was twelve years old, the oldest twenty-one. And that's without counting the attempted kidnapping and rape of three other girls ... The companion of the "ogre of the Ardennes", Monique Olivier, was sentenced to life imprisonment with a security sentence of twenty-eight years for complicity in four of these crimes, and non-indictment of murders. "By her reassuring presence, she would bring down the game, always in a car. She would sometimes clean them, before he raped them, and strangled them." The investigators discover that in prison already, in the years 1980, Michel Fourniret had revealed his criminal projects to Monique Olivier.

Their story began on December 12, 1986, in the pages of the Catholic weekly *Le Pèlerin*, where Monique Olivier had noticed a small advertisement: "Prisoner would like to correspond with a person of any age to forget loneliness. The author was none other than Fourniret, who was then serving a prison sentence in Fleury-Mérogis for sexual assault. Upon his release in October 1987, he moved in with Monique before marrying her a year later. A secret pact had been made in the meantime. In one of his letters, the "ogre of the Ardennes" had outlined his program as follows: "Have enough money to forget about money, liquidate three guys, have a young slot, female company, play chess, live as an adventurer, pleasure of living, kidnapping, etc." In exchange for young virgins, he commits to his correspondent to liquidate three men: his two former companions and the man who once took her virginity.

"I always dreamed of knowing the immaculate", this is what Fourniret said. Worse still, the Olivier-Fourniret couple has a little boy named Selim, who was used as bait, as a baby, to put his victims in confidence. A child described as an "accident" by his mother and little loved by his father. He is the third son of Monique Olivier and the fifth child of the "Ogre of the Ardennes".

Seven victims, at least," continues Christophe Hondelatte, "maybe more! The investigation is not over."

At the time of writing, the investigation is not closed. Every six months, Fourniret's name resurfaces in unsolved cases of murders of young girls and adolescents. There are about fifty unsolved criminal cases on which his shadow hangs, including that of Joanna Parrish, a twenty-year-old British girl, strangled in May 1990 in Auxerre, or that of Marie-Angèle Domèce.

In short, Justice has disconnected the counter of the victims on the number seven. It should be noted that the police found about thirty unknown DNAs on the four thousand hairs that were in the back of his white van, the same one he used to trap his prey.

On October 22, 1987, Michel Fourniret was released from Fleury-Mérogis, despite his profile as a predator with a huge potential for recidivism," warns Christophe Hondelatte. And besides, it will not take long.

In 1989, the ogre and his wife, accompanied by their son Selim, left their dilapidated cottage in Floing in the Ardennes, where they were so miserably entrenched, and took up residence in the sumptuous Château du Sautou, in Donchery, deep in a forest. A castle, nothing less!

The ogre and his wife, with eyes like fried whiting, have taken up residence under the golden panelling of the Château du Sautou, a nineteenth-century manor house flanked by two corner turrets with pointed roofs, located on the Belgian border, in the heart of a property with 15 hectares of forest. The amount spent for its acquisition is 1.2 million francs in cash, the equivalent of 183,000 euros. How did a man described as a simple earth-bound ass succeed in adorning himself with such superb finery?

"It wasn't just the neighbors who were intrigued," the host warns. "In 1990, the anti-terrorist section in Paris and the judicial police in Reims also began to take an interest in Michel Fourniret. How could an ex-convict who lives only on odd jobs buy such a property? The police know that Michel Fourniret knew in prison, in Fleury-Mérogis, Jean-Pierre Hellegouarch, whom they suspect of having links with the extreme left-wing armed movement Action directe. As a result, they wondered whether the Sautou castle might not be a hideout for terrorists. They set up a discreet surveillance of the castle... In 1990, the Justice ordered a search. As a result, Michel Fourniret will have to pay a tax adjustment of forty-three thousand euros. That was all. A year later, in 1992, the Fourniret family abandoned their castle and suddenly moved to Belgium to settle in the village of Sart-Custinne.

According to Christophe Hondelatte, there is another murder, that of a certain Farida Hammiche that the ogre admitted having killed with a bayonet with the help of Monique Olivier, on April 12, 1988. This Farida is none other than the wife of Jean-Pierre Hellegouarch, known as "the Breton", an ex-braker having been the neighbor of cell of Michel Fourniret, in the house of arrest of Fleury-Mérogis, between 1984 and 1987. Relying on surprising revelations published in the newspaper *Libération*, on July 24, 2004, under the pen of Patricia Tourancheau, Christophe Hondelatte pronounces this sentence that I will not soon forget: "Fourniret would have embezzled a part of the Postiches gang's loot."

The Postiches gang? This legendary gang that made headlines by robbing banks around Paris from 1981 to 1986, wearing fake noses, wigs, and masks of the illustrious Georges Marchais? Rather than getting lost in useless paraphrases, here is the famous article in question, soberly entitled " Fourniret a braqué le butin des Postiches ", that my colleague authorized me to reproduce here :

Patricia Tourancheau in *Libération - Once upon a time, there* was a golden hoard, stolen several times from highwaymen, then fell into the dirty hands of Michel Fourniret. The serial killer made a fortune and even bought a castle. It was wrongly mentioned that it was the loot of the terrorist group Action directe (AD) or the proceeds of the robberies of a Breton far left, Jean-Pierre Hellegouarch.

The "serial killer" confessed to having stolen in 1988 "about fifty kilos of gold" buried in a cemetery in the Paris region and killed the girlfriend of Hellegouarch, his former cellmate, who had asked him to transport them to a new hiding place. Questioned two weeks ago, Hellegouarch declared that this "stock of gold" belonged to an Italian convict who, in the process of being extradited, wanted "to get his stock of gold out of its hiding place".

We found the name of this Italian, then incarcerated at Fleury-Mérogis: Gian Luigi Esposito. And this is where his story crosses the Postiches gang. Because this Italian made off in a helicopter from the prison of Rome in company of a member of the gang and took refuge in the Parisian suburbs in the hideout of these bandits. Today we reveal that the murderer from the Ardennes has recovered, by ricochet and without knowing it, the "war chest" of the Postiches gang.

These Robin Hood-like bank robbers, who robbed client safes in the beautiful neighborhoods of Paris, Neuilly and Passy in the 1980s, buried "thirty-four bars and thousands of gold coins next to a grave in a small, quiet cemetery in the Paris region" one night in December 1986, according to Robert Marguery, a former Postiche who became a mystic in Thailand. "There were four of them to bury him. I was already on the ball when it happened. Afterwards, my late teammate Jean-Claude Myszka wanted to give me the location of the hiding place: "I'll tell you where the treasure is stashed in case you get out before me." My mind was elsewhere, I was thinking of going away for life, I never wanted to know the exact location. It's a little gloomy. I wouldn't put my bullion in a cemetery." His Postiches buddies thought the cops would never find their loot in a place like that. The problem is that others found it.

When he was released from prison in 1999, Jean-Claude Myszka, who had not spent a day for thirteen years without thinking about his "treasure", found nothing in Ali Baba's tomb. He has dug and dug and dug, all in vain. No more the least "jaunet". And impossible to file a complaint. "600 to 800 million gold disappeared from the tomb of this cemetery, that's for sure", reports his confidant Marguery. The golden years were over. Poor and desperate, living with his mother in Aubervilliers, Myszka, who was once rich, fell apart, obsessed by the loss of his gold. Did a gravedigger or a gardener "by chance" stumble upon the loot? Worse, did one of the three others who shared the secret betray it? Myszka begins to doubt the two Postiches, as well as the "Italian escapee", Gian Luigi Esposito, who accompanied her when she buried the gold.

They were four hidden in a house in Yerres (Essonne). At the end of the twenty-seventh robbery in five years, thousands of safes opened with a hammer and chisel, these gangsters from Belleville and Montreuil, who dressed up as bourgeois - loden and cashmere, designer suits, British hats, with wigs and fake moustaches -, fell on January 14, 1986 at the exit of the Crédit Lyonnais in the rue du Docteur-Blanche in Paris (XVIth). A shootout with the police killed a gangster and a detective. Marguery was arrested. The three survivors of the Postiches crossed the Alps on skis. They spend a peaceful retirement in Rome. But one of them, André Bellaïche, was arrested by the carabinieri on August 5, 1986 for a traffic violation and imprisoned in Rebibbia with the mafiosi, the Red Brigades and the Black Shirts.

The faithful Myszka and a second pillar of the gang flew to his rescue with a Red Cross helicopter. On November 23, 1986, André Bellaïche, an anarchist by nature, escaped from the prison yard with a fellow inmate: Gian Luigi Esposito, a bank robber linked to the Italian extreme right. The four fugitives return to France in a "gold Lancia" and hide out in the Paris suburbs. The police tracked down the address - 28, rue des Pins in Yerres (Essonne) - and monitored the villa. The investigators identified four men who left the house on December 11, 1986 at 1:10 p.m. and got into the car: Gian Luigi Esposito, in a yellow and black striped scarf, at the wheel, and Jean-Claude Myszka in the passenger seat; André Bellaïche and Patrick Geay, another Postiche, dressed like princes, in the back. They drove to Villeneuve-Saint-Georges (Val-de-Marne), then towards Paris. The policemen "stop the tailing by measure of discretion". The suspects return to Yerres at 22 h 35. It is probably this evening that the bandits transport the exhumed "treasure" from its hiding place, to bury it on the grave of an unknown person in a country cemetery.

The Raid arrested the four bandits on December 13, 1986. The criminal brigade raided the walls of the house, which had been perforated like a Swiss cheese by Myszka, and found more than 6,000 gold coins and kilos of jewelry. But no gold bars!

Meanwhile, in Fleury-Mérogis, Jean-Pierre Hellegouarch, imprisoned for drug trafficking and armed robbery, shares his cell with a certain Michel Fourniret, a "pointer" who raped teenage girls. From 1984 to 1987, the two convicts had time to become friends. Fourniret leaves the first, in October 1987, leaves his address of Saint-Cyr-les-Colons in Yonne to his fellow prisoner, continues to write to him and to "assist him". Then Hellegouarch discovered a good lead, "in March 1988" according to his recent statements to the judicial police in Versailles: "I met in Fleury an

Italian wanted in Italy for an escape by helicopter from the Rebibbia prison belonging to an extreme right-wing movement and who had a stock of gold in a cemetery in the Paris region." He specifies that this Italian in the process of being extradited asks him to "help him take the money out of the place" in exchange for a commission. On his report, Hellegouarch never mentions the name of the Italian. He does not remember it. The investigators do not insist, convinced that it is an invention to mask the origin of a personal booty.

Now we have unmasked this Italian who fits the description provided by Hellegouarch. There are only two escapees from Rebibbia prison by helicopter. Gian Luigi Esposito inaugurated in 1986 with André Bellaïche this type of escape baptized in Italy *a la francese* and attended the burial of the "treasure" of the Postiches. This week, the Versailles Police Station verified our hypothesis: Gian Luigi Esposito was indeed held at Fleury-Mérogis from December 15, 1986 to April 12, 1988, at the same time as Jean-Pierre Hellegouarch and Michel Fourniret. Since then, the investigators have been trying to get their hands on Esposito and are considering rehearing Hellegouarch.

According to his first hearing, Hellegouarch agrees, in March 1988, to give a hand to his Italian co-detainee, via his companion Farida Hammiche and a good friend on whom one can count, Fourniret. In the next visiting room, the Breton informs Farida of the mission to be accomplished, tells her the exact location of the ingots' hiding place, "at the back of a grave in a marble planter", and instructs her to contact "Michel" in the Yonne to ask him for this service, in exchange for "a bonus of five hundred thousand francs or the purchase of a farm". So the Ardennais and

Farida set off on a trip to the famous cemetery. They recovered "about fifty kilos of gold", according to Fourniret's confession, and then "transferred" the heavy load to the apartment of Farida and her partner (still incarcerated), in Vitry in the Val-de-Marne. Fourniret, who knows a lot about masonry and carpentry, even built a hiding place above the door of the couple's toilet and stuffed the entire loot inside. In the two weeks that follow, Fourniret changes his mind and forms a dark plan.

According to the minutes of his confession, he persuaded Farida to come with him to "look for weapons in Rambouillet", a pretext to lure her to his land in Clairefontaine (Yvelines). He kills Farida, puts her body in his car and "drives around all day" before burying her "at the exit of a village in the Yvelines, at the bottom of a slope", according to his vague and questionable statements. He did not forget to steal "half of the gold stock" from the cache he had just cobbled together. He claims that he left the other half in Hellegouarch's apartment in Vitry. After the "disappearance" of Farida, on April 12, 1988, the day of Esposito's extradition, Fourniret sympathized with the sorrow of his ex-cellmate, participated in the search with the family and even employed a private detective to find the young woman. Released on October 15, 1988, Hellegouarch only collected "200,000 francs in gold coins" in the cache of his house in Vitry. He suspects a little Fourniret of the theft of the loot and the death of Farida. He hurried to visit him in the Ardennes. Monique and "Michel" receive him in their house in Floing, and make him the blow of poverty. The Breton leaves, reassured. He does not suspect that Fourniret changed the ingots in Belgium, the coins at numismatists, to buy the castle of Sautou in Donchery (Ardennes), plus an apartment in Sedan and a new van. Then, in 1991, Hellegouarch learned by chance of the acquisition of the Sautou estate because of a small investigation by the Paris criminal brigade on a story of false papers. Fourniret's castle was searched. This address appears on the procedure that reaches... Hellegouarch. Furious at having been "double-crossed", Hellegouarch went to ask Fourniret for an explanation. Hellegouarch fires a shot at the "traitor", threatens his wife - Monique Olivier - with a gun placed to her head. To escape Hellegouarch's possible revenge, the Fournirets immediately sold the mansion and moved to Belgium, to Sart-Custinne. According to Monique Fourniret, who, on June 29, denounced her husband to the Belgian police for ten crimes, the murder of Farida Hammiche is similar to a "settlement of accounts" on the part of her husband, in order to "recover the gold he was supposed to share" with Hellegouarch's companion.

Of the Postiches' treasure, betrayed by Esposito who used Hellegouarch, himself robbed by the Ardennes serial killer, only the equivalent of 25,000 euros in Spanish, Canadian and Mexican coins and gold louis remain, found at the beginning of July in a washing machine buried by Fourniret in Belgium.

Le Postiche Jean-Claude Myszka died at the age of forty-seven on February 11, 2003, penniless and insane, sick of this lost "treasure" that he tracked down without ever finding a trace.

***

In short, the "ogre of the Ardennes" stole a pirate treasure and then celebrated his achievement by taking the

crown of the Sautou. I can only bow to such mafia genius…
More importantly, if he hadn't touched any children, this
miserable jerk might still be on the throne. There are,
indeed, all the signs of a romantic predisposition, which
distinguishes, in my opinion, the Fourniret case from all
the other tragedies in five acts. Obviously, it is not only
a vile being who throws himself wholeheartedly into the
practice of pedophilia. He is first and foremost a thunder-
bolt of formidable intelligence.

As the program drew to a close, Christophe Hondelatte
walked past a red Genoese wall with portraits of the two
suspects and concluded, "Their son has, since the affair,
changed his name. He now lives with the two older sons of
Monique Olivier, in the south of France."

Taking a coffee as black as a bottomless pit, I realize
the content of the information that has just been given to
me. Selim Fourniret, the son of the ogre - who has never
given a single interview - would live close to me. I jump up
and start to search on the Web. In five minutes, the trick
is done. Five minutes! That's how long it took me to find
the Fourniret son on a famous social network. In addition
to the new name to which he answers, all the information
agrees with those contained in his family booklet, which
I could consult in a hurry by a diverted way:

"On the ninth of September nineteen hundred and
eighty-eight at eleven o'clock, Selim Gwenaël Jean-Pierre
was born, 45, avenue de Manchester in Charleville-Mézières,
of the male sex, to Michel Paul Fourniret, born on the 4th
of April 1942 in Sedan, in the Ardennes, a draughtsman by
profession, and Monique Pierrette Olivier, born on the 31st
of October 1948 in Tours, in the Indre-et-Loire region, of
no profession, domiciled in Floing, rue du Rossignol, who

declare that they recognise him. Drawn up on September tenth, nineteen hundred and eighty-eight at ten hours and forty minutes, on the declaration of the father and mother."

As further proof of his identity, I have just found the portrait of a young man of twenty-five years of age who corresponds in every way to the profile sought. I have the impression of having the emaciated face of the "ogre" in front of me, covered with the facial graft of Monique Olivier. He poses next to a man wearing a small medallion on his shirt in the shape of a red iron cross, widely used by the Third Reich. This is a symbol of Nazi Germany. What should we expect from the son of a pedophile murderer, who made the news? Who knows, if I were him, I might have fallen into extremism myself...

At 3:39 p.m., I send this email to his attention:

Me, *to Selim Fourniret* - Hello, my name is Oli. I understand that you live in the Alpes-Maritimes. I would like to know if you would agree to meet me in order to offer you a platform in the press. Of course, your new identity will remain confidential, and you will have, moreover, a right of control on the contents before publication. I think it will be important to emphasize your achievement of having made it through a difficult childhood. What do you think about it?

2.

SELIM

January 29, 2014

My message will remain a dead letter until January 29, 2014, when I stay at a friend's house in Geneva. I'm staying at his place. Straight down from heaven at the sound of noon, the son of the ogre sends me the following text message:

Selim. - Sorry to respond so late to your gracious request. The feat of getting away with it? Let's just say it's all a facade. I didn't really have a choice. I owe my life only to my fear of suicide. I'm just a coward.

Me. - **Not everyone** can find the courage to survive, believe me. I speak from experience. By the way, we are neighbors. I live in Nice. What day of the week could we meet to discuss all this in person?

Selim. - We can meet, no problem. I work at night. I am available every day, at your convenience.

Me. - I guess I'm not the first System Guy to ask you. Why me?

Selim. - We are almost the same age. You are the youngest journalist to have contacted me, that's all.

Me. - In that case, let's be on first-name terms! Would next Tuesday suit you?

Selim. - Okay, no worries.

I leave Switzerland, without giving myself the time to share with my worthy friend a final plate of *penne alla carbonara*, at the mythical Café de la Presse, located fifty meters from the Cemetery of the Kings, where the eminent Jorge Luis Borges lies.

In Nice, at the beginning of February, on a Tuesday, I met Selim for the first time, by a beautiful sunny afternoon, at the bottom of the big crossing which gives on the Garibaldi place! It was 2:33 pm.

"Hello, nice to meet you, Selim," I said, grabbing his outstretched hand.

- Very honored," he answers, taciturn, enveloping me with his dull gaze.

- Thank you for agreeing to the meeting.

- Come on, it's only natural."

To my astonishment, Selim claims not to be interested in the business that bears his former name. In fact, he has not mentioned it for ten years, not even with his half-brothers, Wendel and Marvin[1]. He ignores everything, until the divorce of his parents pronounced by the judge of the family affairs of Charleville-Mézières, on July 2, 2010. "Drinking a lot of strong coffee, he confesses, is the best way to stop dreaming about them. Caffeine causes sleep disorders that

---

1. The first names were changed at Selim's request, in the name of protecting the privacy of his relatives.

stop the memory mechanism. You see, I refuse to see them again in a dream. Never again". The humoristic radio station Rire et Chansons remains his only source of information.

Selim seems at first sight to be a character closed on himself, with a slender size, reaching six feet two inches, thanks to long legs contrasting with a small bust engulfed in a blue polo shirt eliminated, and a huge noggin shaved with a serrated blade. He's not a skinhead. "I didn't expect to see you dressed like that, in such a classic way." And for good reason, in 2008, a strange lisp spread in the press, claiming to be the one and only journalist who had the privilege of interviewing him, pushing the attention to detail to describe him as "a young man always wearing a rapper's cap."

Pfff!", Selim blows with a weary air, sweeping the subject away with a wave of his hand. This guy... A forger! He has never written anything but rubbish about me. He has never, ever been my confidant. And what else? All this is pure invention of his own. And, very slightly, he adds: "I hate rap."

Selim and I rush into the old antique district through a maze of alleys, and end up dropping anchor in a pirates' den. It's a small drinking establishment, which the regulars call the Almira Wobben[2]. Most of the customers are English-speaking thirst-quenchers. They speak so loudly that it gives the illusion of being elsewhere...

Selim collapses on a black chair covered with leather. His voice betrays a certain fatigue. After six years as a waiter, he is now a night watchman in a perfume factory near Grasse.

Me, *softly* - How do you live this cursed heritage?

---

2. Fictitious name.

Selim. - It is very hard to bear. I think about it very often during moments of solitude. It haunts me, especially at Christmas time, when everyone gathers with their families. I never talk about it anyway, not even with my brothers. Only three or four of my friends know about my past. When people ask me what my parents do for a living, I usually answer, "They're dead." I know I will never see them again. My father was sentenced to life in prison and I seriously doubt that my mother will make it out alive. If she does, she will be in very bad shape anyway. Whatever happens, as I said, my parents are already dead to me.

Me. - Ten years ago, you expressed the wish to see your mother again. What happened?

Selim, *with a big heartache* - I really wanted to. Except that, at that time, the police had not yet shed any light on the details of the case. I had no idea that they had both used me as a baby to lure their victims, including Elisabeth Brichet, in 1989. Since then, my mother has become a stranger. By helping my father to commit his crimes, she clearly made her choice. She could have very well not followed him in his delirium, and left him. But she didn't! She helped him. This is unforgivable. Therefore, I chose not to have to put up with her anymore, something I made clear to her in my very last letter. She did not insist.

Me, *lowering my head to read my notes* - Do you remember the day you learned the truth about your father?

Selim. - It was the day of his arrest, June 26, 2003. I was then fourteen years old. I had just returned from a school trip to Alsace. My mother had picked me up from school. On the way back, she said to me: "Your father is not here. He won't be back for a while." At the same time, I saw a row of police cars parked outside our house in Sart-

Custinne, Belgium. I immediately asked my mother what was going on. "Your father is gone," she repeated, embarrassed. It was while watching TV that I finally understood. When I heard about the robberies, I thought that maybe I was the son of a gangster. When I realized that he wasn't coming home anytime soon, I felt joy inside. I didn't like my father...

Me. - In 2004, your mother, who was still free, denounced Michel Fourniret and accused him of ten murders. Did you play a role in these confessions?

Selim. - She soon realized that I was happy that he was not there. My father has an overwhelming personality. Without him, we could finally breathe at home. It was perfect. Maybe that's what convinced her to confess. Then he blamed me for his last kidnapping attempt, on Marie-Ascension, in Ciney, Belgium. He told the investigators, "I did this because my son had given me a bad report card that morning." I was very bad at school. But imagine the shock! Beyond that, I think my mother, who is psychologically fragile, would have confessed everything with or without me.

Me. - On June 28, 2004, Monique Olivier was arrested in her turn for complicity in crimes. What happened to you then?

Selim, *frowning* - The police were never there for me. When officers came to arrest my mother in Waulsort, they said they had to take her to the station to ask her some questions. But she never came back. I was left alone at home. I was just a fifteen year old kid. I was terrified. The public prosecutor of Dinant had simply forgotten about me, neglecting to take care of me through the youth assistance service.

Me. - Dinant? Well, what's the surprise? I read somewhere that this commune was twinned with the Disneyland Paris park, in December 2013. So, what to expect from such a bunch of Mickeys? Well, what happened next?

Selim, *painfully* - After a week, André, my paternal uncle, finally came to get me and took me to his house in Sedan. There, he just told me: "Your mother will not come back. He thought he would get rid of me as soon as possible, planning to enroll me in boarding school or military school. He said he did not want to take in the son of a criminal - "*who is surely the same* [as his father]". At the beginning of July 2004, my half-brother on my mother's side showed up without warning. I still don't know how he knew where to find me, but he appeared and said, "Selim, we're leaving! In no time at all, we were on our way to the French Riviera. He drove me to his home in Vallauris. At the age of twenty-three, he became my legal guardian. Before that, I had only seen him three or four times. The fact is that he did not get along with my father at all. He was my savior! When I arrived at his house, he immediately introduced me to sports. Thanks to him, I quickly got back into my studies by pursuing a second year of CAP catering, in Cagnes-sur-Mer. Afterwards, I even obtained a professional baccalaureate, in Menton. All this story will have at least had the merit to have made me fall into the real world.

Me. - What came before?

Selim. - My life with mom and dad, a fake universe where everything seemed to be fine and rosy. I lived in a lie for most of my life. To tell you the truth, for a long time I was angry at myself for having been so naive. I knew that my dad was not as cool as the dads of my classmates who always took the time to play with them. Mine was an angry man who spent most of his time working around the house. I had to accompany him in his tasks. Nevertheless, all this seemed normal to me. I had never known anything else.

Me. - Has he ever been violent towards you?

Selim. - No, it never went beyond the stage of a threat.

Me. - Michel Fourniret never hid his obsession with the Virgin Mary. So why did he give you a Muslim name?

Selim. - He called me that in homage to a robber who shared his cell at Fleury-Mérogis. I am named after a convict. And as if that wasn't enough, he then chose as my godfather the bank robber Jean-Pierre Hellegouarch!

Me. - In a document submitted to the trial court, your father described himself as "an evil being devoid of any human feeling, worse than Dutroux". Does this definition fit him?

Selim. - Everyone has feelings. As proof, when his other son, Nicolas, died on December 29, 1995 in Normandy, caught by a wood chipper, the sky fell on his head. He was devastated, even crying his eyes out. My father may have presented himself as a cold individual with a high IQ, but he was still a human being.

Me, *leaning in* - Do you think, like the police, that he could still be linked to unsolved murders?

Selim, *completely baffled* - It's quite possible! I'm sure he didn't confess everything...

Me, *then, lower* - In 1989, your family acquires the castle of Sautou, in the Ardennes, a property of fifteen hectares bought in cash, thanks to the loot of the Postiches gang. Do you have any memory of it?

Selim, *thoughtful* - What I remember is that there was a lot of money in the house. It was pompously displayed there... Besides, some gold louis from this booty would still be stashed underground. My mother would have hidden some after the arrest of my father...

***

To think that we still dare to complain about our little worries... Selim's survival is a great and beautiful lesson of life, that we should all take into consideration to relativize a bit.

The day falls. Selim and I leave it at that, but we promise to meet again soon. We had no idea that we would spend three whole years at the Almira Wobben, once or twice a week. Three years of adventure, in pursuit of the forgotten treasure of the Postiches, the gang that once taunted the socialist government.

3.
THE OGRE APPEARS

February 2, 2014

By an incredible twist of fate, I learned that the "Ogre of the Ardennes" had suddenly appeared before the prince, and in writing, the next day. Michel Fourniret regains the use of speech after a decade of profound mutism. And suddenly Selim starts to suspect me of having made a deal with his father, of working for him.

Don't you think it's weird?" he says, without looking up. Nothing for nine years and bim! It resurfaces as if by magic the day after we meet.

- Hey! What do I have to do with all this? First, tell me... Do you believe in fate, Selim?

The son of the "ogre of the Ardennes" shows me an epistle full of antics addressed to him from the prison of Ensisheim, in Alsace:

Michel Fourniret, *to Selim* - It is never too late to do good. In this case, to help Selim Gwenaël Jean-Pierre, my youngest son, on a material level, via a monthly money order. Would it seem unwelcome, or inappropriate, this kind of reconnection after years without the slightest sign of life?

However, that the synergy can make a case that convinces you to say "Bof... O.K. to receive this!" may not be just an illusion. That's for you, Selim, and you alone to decide. Impasse des Maisons-Blanches. Route de Paincourt. Jaws welded, guts tied, cascades of tears, on the side of the eyes. Hello the... sniffles. The emotion. The happiness. The pride!
Subsidiary reason: I should part with a treasure. A treasure without a name that would make all the bankers on the planet die of envy! Message over.

***

A treasure? "A treasure without a name to make all the bankers on the planet die of envy. According to a source close to the case, Michel Fourniret is probably referring to the remains of the Postiches gang's hoard. Rue de Paincourt? Impasse des Maisons-Blanches? When you think about it, it sounds like a treasure hunt. What for? And why? The more I think about it, the more I am convinced that it can only be a clever allusion to the remains of 34 ingots, and thousands of gold coins...
An article by Marc Metdepenningen, published in the Belgian daily *Le Soir* on April 1st, 2008, describes how the judicial police of Dinant set up a trap for the "Diaboliques" by installing bugs in the "unsupervised visit" room, with the agreement of an investigating judge. During their meetings, Monique Olivier and Michel Fourniret had "worked out a defense strategy together. They were worried about what would happen next," says Dinant police inspector Stéphane

Brasseur. The police then tried a thousand tricks, going so far as to place microphones in the private rooms of the Dinant prison. Monique Olivier, free, regularly visited her husband. These eavesdropping sessions taught them a lot, especially about the existence of a hidden booty.

"During these interviews, Monique Olivier shared her fears with Fourniret: "I don't know if I will still be free in June. He reassures her: "Remain evasive in your statements", he advises her. They talk about the treasure, which they only refer to with periphrases such as "the brunos" or "the little ones". These are the coins and gold bars from the Postiches gang's loot, which Monique Olivier buried after her husband's arrest [...] After Fourniret's arrest, Monique recovered the balance of the loot: some twenty-five thousand euros in gold louis and Spanish currency.

From that day on, Michel Fourniret will occupy a growing place in my life.

I will be obsessed with the serial killing couple and will search for the rest of the Postiches' loot, along with Selim, for almost three years.

With the son of the "ogre", we went to see *The Last Gang* by Ariel Zeitoun. This cinematographic work retraces the eventful itinerary of the Postiches gang in the "Belleville of the Jews and Arabs, the demonstrations of the filthy backyards". Of course, all this is told in a very romantic way, but the facts are there.

As indicated in the exhibition scene, "this film is, in part, freely inspired by the story of André Bellaïche, and certain facts of which he was accused, and of which he was acquitted". I will soon have to meet him.

All the interest of this film lies in its final scene, during which it is announced that the gang's treasure has vanished.

After leaving a bank, the character of Simon, a cheeky and inventive robber played by Vincent Elbaz, finds his wife in front of a carousel. He swears that he has retired from the business. In a sepulchral atmosphere, full of nostalgia, he concludes: "With my friends, when we got out of prison, we wanted to recover the money we had stashed away, but everything had disappeared, like in a nightmare. Even if nobody suspected anyone, we never saw each other again. There's not a minute when I don't think about them, the living and the dead."

***

Fourniret, this name is never pronounced... Selim, on discovering this scene closely linked - in a way - to his own childhood, would have said: "Hey! but, it's Mich-Mich who took everything! It's a really good film. At the end, when it is announced that the treasure is gone, I couldn't help but crack a mocking smile!"

Selim can no longer feign ignorance. All these sums amassed in an overabundant way with great blows of hammer, chisel, crowbar, crowbar, and what do I know? 27 bank branches! 1,300 safety deposit boxes! Now he knows.

My interview with Selim Fourniret will be published on March 20, 2014, in the columns of *VSD*. A version somewhat redacted, on the grounds that the casual tone used by the Prince of Sautou was likely to affect the Belgian authorities[3]. On the title page of the magazine there is a yellow band around the dislocated hips of Bernadette Chirac - presented here as "la tata flingueuse" - on which it is written: "Michel Fourniret, his son speaks for the first time: Mes parents sont morts."

---

3. *VSD* No. 1908, March 20-26, 2014.

4.
THE PRINCE WITHOUT A KINGDOM

"Everything is repugnant, when one betrays one's nature
to commit a vile action."
Sophocles

April 4, 2014, in Nice

At about 6 p.m. on the port of Nice, as I was leaving Selim, the Prince of Sautou, I asked him if he had already accepted or refused any succession. At these words, a shadow passes over his face, until then impassive.

Yes, alas!" he answers at the top of his lungs, admiring at sunset a white liner gliding towards the Island of Beauty.

- Ah, that's a long story, and I wouldn't want to bore you with it...

- No, no, I'm interested.

- My inheritance, Selim continues, well, it is limited to shame... A shame that has never diminished with time. Basically, I was supposed to receive by right of succession the stone house of Sart-Custinne, and a small piece of land.

Michel had put them in my name to avoid me ending up under the bridge, knowing that they would both end up sinking, sooner or later. But that too, they were taken from me..."

On this subject, he sends me an old missive from prisoner n° 5451, addressed to his second wife, Nicole, from the time he was in detention at the Châlons-en-Champagne prison. Michel Fourniret feels obliged to specify - by letter dated November 30, 2007, that is to say four months before the opening of his trial - that the only beneficiary of the Sart-Custinne house is his son Selim.

Michel Fourniret, *to Nicole* - Did I already tell you? My memory being faulty, it would be selfish of me not to run the risk of repeating it, to remind you that since the beginning, the house of Sart-Custinne is the property, or bare ownership as educated people say, of Selim. About Selim: now that he seems to be in the South of France, it is likely that my son, who has reached the age of legal majority since September 9, 2007, will decide to sell this house which, at present, only brings me road tax notices in my mailbox.

***

If my parents bought the house in Sart-Custinne in my name," Selim continues, staring at the thick black smoke of a large liner, "it is not for altruism. It was a classic move. It was a question of taking measures to avoid any risk of seizure, in the event of continuations. Nevertheless, the justice system put the house under seal for the duration of the investigation. It was quickly shown that my parents had already committed misdeeds before buying it, not to mention that the money for its purchase came from a theft... They got rich at the expense of others, by pilfering. The judge thus considered that it was an organized fraud aiming at harming a future creditor, and thus escaping any pecuniary responsibility. After eight years, considering that Mich-Mich had voluntarily reduced the value of his patrimony knowingly, and thus evaded the tax, the Justice concluded that my title of property had to succumb under the Paulian action. This is how this old decrepit building was sold at auction before a notary for the modest sum of 57,000 euros. This year, it was resold for 50,000 euros. A derisory price!

Add to that the fact that this "battery of pigeons[4]" was condemned in 2008 to pay the round sum of 1,039,740 euros as compensatory damages to the 37 civil parties. When the judge called, the coffers had to be replenished. An allegedly insolvent criminal was indeed condemned to pay more than 1 million euros to the victims' families!

"Is this not indirect proof of the existence of a treasure? For how else can your father hope to find so much money, except by drawing on the resources of the Postiches?

- No, you're not," says Selim. The amount of damages is not proportional to personal assets. It is set according to the harm suffered, which includes the financial losses caused by the crimes.

The sun gradually disappears behind the crest of the hill. As the twilight mixes in the arms of Nyx the cold becomes more and more teasing. The chin pressed on the thorax, Selim sketches a smile. With our return, with the triple gallop, at the door of the sign of Almira Wobben, where

---

4. In police language, this refers to a couple accused of the same facts.

we had spent all the afternoon, we reinstall ourselves near the fire. As soon as we are seated in front of an appetizing scramble of eggs with bacon, Selim continues in the same tone: "Contrary to what has been said in the press, I never wanted this damned barrack! I never answered the summonses. Never! However, I still needed the money to rebuild myself... But that's the way the law is. Now you know why Michel pays me a tribute by money order. In fact, he refuses to let all his money go to the victims' relatives. To the end, he will not have respected them.

Coming back to the legacy of shame, in 2012 I went back to Belgium, to Sart-Custinne, to visit friends, still dear to my heart. Out of pure curiosity, I had made a detour to our old house, located at 18 rue de Vencimont. There, I fell into the nets of a policeman asking me maliciously what I had come to do in the corner. When I was spotted in the distance, a neighbor reported my presence to the authorities, convinced that I was there to cover up evidence. I felt humiliated, rejected. What a shame!

Two weeks later, when the time came to scatter us to the four winds, Selim, slumped by drunkenness, slipped his hand into his beige canvas bissac, emptying it of its victuals, to keep only one object.

"To answer your question of the other day... I thought long and hard... That's all I have left. Ah, but where did it go?" He pulls out a photograph of himself in a school situation. "Never anything but a few oxidized grains on kerosene..."

This portrait taken in 1993 is striking! Selim was five years old at the time, when he was attending the kindergarten in the village of Sart-Custinne, the same one where Michel Fourniret worked as a supervisor in the canteen...

All the wounds of the soul, of the heart, of the mind are written on this young face. Is it a call for help? His grey-blue eyes are imbued with a dark and abysmal sadness. A disturbing coincidence: with his beatnik hairstyle and his little red checkered shirt, this little boy with diaphanous skin looks like a modern incarnation of the character of Danny in Stanley Kubrick's film *Shining*. In this film, the child of light finds himself trapped between the four icy walls of an isolated palace in the Rocky Mountains, in the presence of a father possessed by the death instinct. And what about the Grady twins who haunt the hotel corridors, reminiscent of Selim, Anne and the late Marie-Hélène? The latter committed suicide on February 21, 2006, ashamed of her father's crimes. I imagine Selim in blue overalls, riding a tricycle slowly down a maze of corridors in the very rupin castle of Sautou, with its floor covered with a carpet embroidered with curious geometric interlacing reminding of this labyrinth in which he would have been lost, like Theseus facing the Minotaur, to whom young virgins were offered...

"When you leave school, who usually picks you up? Monique or Michel?

- No one," replied Selim, shaking his head forcefully. The school was on the corner of Vencimont Street, a few steps from our house. So I walked there.

- But what a horror! Poor little guy...

- Since childhood, I have been independent.

- Well, I'm outraged, you see! Damn, you were only five years old! At least tell me that someone helped you get dressed in the morning...

- I'll have you know, Oli, that I used to wash, dress, and go to and from school alone, always alone. I had

4. The Prince without a Kingdom

no hope of getting help. I had no hope of getting help. Michel was not the kind of father who would stoop to such menial tasks."

As he leaves, he hands me a yellowed envelope, from which a sheet of crumpled correspondence pad protrudes. "I also found this... It's my mother's last letter, dated May 8, 2007, after three years spent in the Valenciennes prison. Having changed her address afterwards, it was never possible for her to write to me again. It's a miracle I didn't tear it up. Bye-bye."

Monique Olivier, *to Selim* - Hello my dear Selim. With the time and the speed of the mail, I received your postcards last Friday. I am very happy to hear from you and to see that you have not forgotten me. When you receive this letter, you will surely be back on the continent. I have learned from Mrs. Charlet that your visitation permit for May 10 and 11 has been postponed, as those are the dates when you take your baccalaureate. I wish you success, if you like the profession you are preparing for, and if you have a few hours of practice with all the internships you have done, don't let that stop you from doing some revision on the subjects where you are most vulnerable... But it's going well. You'll get it. Just keep me in the loop. Especially in this profession, you have to show that you're confident.

Explain to me after high school, how many years do you have left in internships and school? Will you still be at the same address as you are now? During the vacations? Do you have any internships planned? Let me know if you have any time off. How is your housing problem going? Are you obliged to leave the premises or can you keep your studio during the summer? In other words, is your studio only available to you during the school year? And then, do you have to reapply? Or do you have it for the whole year?

I see that you had a rather exhausting internship in Corsica. You had a very busy schedule, so I'm not surprised that you were knocked out. I hope that you are well paid, because there the tourists are on vacation all year round. It's a shame you were turned down in Canada. Do you think you can go back? How come you didn't have a work contract? Who provides it? Is it the organizer of the internship? Did everything go well for this forced return to France? Is it your educator's fault that you ended up in this situation? Were you accompanied by someone from your school? Did you get the internship in Corsica quickly?

That's a lot of questions, I know, but I'm interested. I'm watching over you from afar, don't worry. Mrs. Charlet warned me about the book that has just come out, and so did my lawyer. We were thinking of having the sale of the book forbidden and of attacking the journalist, as well as M.F., because it is him who is at the origin of all this. Moreover, this book was made illegally. It is forbidden to make books about a case in the middle of an investigation. In principle, everything is and must remain secret. My lawyer assured me that the families of the victims have filed a complaint and are asking for a publication ban. That's good.

I told Mrs. Charlet that she should talk to my lawyers, because I have not contacted any journalists, nor have I met this kind of character. Above all, don't think that I'm responsible for everything that the journalists say. They often call. The lawyers remain discreet about the case. Don't do anything without talking to me. I'll tell you right now that I asked you to say as little as possible, and not to do anything about the questions about us. If she mentions our birth certificates, our address and our schedule, I say again and again that I have nothing to do with the publication of the book. I learned about it from inmates who had shown me an article that had appeared in the newspapers. I gave the article to Mrs. Charlet who must have shared it with your educators. The content of the article is more or less this: Mr. Faussaire asked M.F.'s lawyers for information about his life before he met me, and about his life with me. The lawyers replied: "Ask her by writing to her". Which she did. The correspondence between M.F. and the journalist lasted eighteen months, which led to the creation of the book, but I was not aware of what was going on between them.

My lawyer, Richard Delgenes, had to write to your brothers to explain the truth. Wendel and Marvin accuse me of being the author of the books. They will even imagine that I receive royalties... This is false. M.F. may get some, but not me. Wendel goes so far as to ask me to repair the damage caused to you, asking me to give them the benefit of the royalties, which would allow me to regain their forgiveness. They ask me to apologize. I answered them what I just told you, and that I didn't have any more work in the prison, that I applied for a job on the line, which would give me a hundred euros a month. There goes my ghostwriter's fee. I am no longer in restoration, and since the list of applications for shop work is long, I am not about to get paid.

When you come, above all, arrive at the entrance of the prison at least thirty minutes in advance, otherwise, if you arrive even one minute late, you will not be able to enter. For clothes and shoes, I need them indeed, but as I will be transferred another time for the time of my trial, and then

I will be transferred to a detention center for long sentences - I don't know where yet - it is better to wait. As soon as I am in the detention center, I will give you my address, but we are not there yet. I think there will even be a possibility to phone. For now, we'll have to make do. It's very nice of you to offer to send me some money. I could use it, but I don't want you to go without for me. I'm going to copy you a passage from the rules of the prison:

"Who manages my money? As soon as I arrive, an account is opened in my name in the accounting department, which manages my money. The money I carry and the money sent to me are deposited in this account. Sending money by mail is strictly forbidden, but I can receive money orders. If the Post Office asks you to send a money order, you write my full name, my prison number: 29421E, cell 10.

It's good news to hear that you no longer have the name M.F. It's already one less thing for you to worry about. The one you have chosen is very common. I am looking forward to your next letter with your pictures. I would like you to tell me frankly if you get along well with your brothers. This is not a reproach, it is to confirm an idea I have. In his letter, Wendel was very hard on me. I received another one from Marvin in July 2006. He was not soft either. Maybe I am wrong, which I hope with all my heart. I am not asking you to get angry with them, on the contrary. I would like you to be welded, all three. They look after you. That's a good thing. You can count on them, but it could be that the understanding that reigns between you at the beginning has slackened a little...

If something is wrong, tell me and talk to your educator. Don't be separate from them. Accept to go out with them, from time to time. I see from the postcards that Corsica is beautiful. The restaurant looks nice. Did you stay there or did you have a room outside the hotel? It's great that you went skiing. Where was it in the Alps? Of course you'll go back next year. Maybe you'll fall off less. I've never been skiing. It must be impressive the first time. Was there much snow? How high is the resort? I'll decorate my cell with the maps. It will make me dream a little, and get closer to you. I hope that you will receive this letter quickly, that it will not take a year to reach you.

I remind you for the visit to the prison of Valenciennes: be present for half an hour at the entrance, with your identity papers, visit permit, and especially leave your cell phone and don't forget to turn it off. Do not carry any metallic object.

As soon as Mrs. Charlet has your visit dates, I will communicate them to my lawyers, who will notify the judge to request a double visit. I hope to see you soon for a visit. I'm waiting to hear from you. I give you a big hug - Mom.

***

This letter is edifying as to the maternal instinct that Monique Olivier has for Selim. Unlike Fourniret - whom she calls by his initials, as if she feared that he would appear at the mere mention of his name - she shows an unconcealed concern for Selim. But there is a catch in the way she mentions her two other sons, Marvin and Wendel, whom they suspect of cruelty towards Selim, who assures me that he does not know what she is referring to. It seems to me that this reverses the assumption that Monique Olivier was under the influence of men, however fierce they may have been. I can't help but think that she has put some malice into this letter, and that she too is a clever manipulator...

This will be, moreover, the one and only letter from Monique Olivier.

"The wretch! My mother was not always a prisoner of the ogre. Nothing forced her to do so," says Selim, who spits on my iron shoes. Far from it. She's not a moron, contrary to what her lawyer would have us believe. To me, she has always seemed normal. But it's as clear as day. Yes! She put herself in this position by sealing a pact with him, to have her ex-husband killed, the father of my half-brothers: André Michaut, the same one who kindly took me in under his roof, in Vallauris, in July 2004. According to her, he beat her.

Before giving herself body and soul to the "ogre of the Ardennes," Monique Olivier lived for ten years with André Michaux, a blackfoot with a white beard, with whom she had two children, Wendel and Marvin. "Everything I said, I maintain it," Monique Olivier maintained during the trial. "That he hit me all night, that he slapped me, spat in my face and tried to strangle me... You pulled me by the mat to the bathtub... He plunged my head under water... He told me that this was how they made the Arabs talk in Algeria..."

Selim does not know if it is the truth, especially since the doctors agreed to say that Monique Olivier did not suffer from a depressive state, nor psychotic, and even less neurotic. "Even if she presents herself almost as a victim of Fourniret, she is not subjected to her husband", had even assured the Ardennes psychiatrist, Paul Belveze.

Knowing that poor André was an art lover," Selim continues, "Mich-Mich went so far as to set fire to his paintings in 1987 at the express request of "Mother", making his life a ordeal for sixteen years. Moreover, "Mother" knew very well what to expect when she married an infernal convict who had already been sentenced for pedophilia. For all these reasons, I will never forgive her. Never!"

A psychiatrist once put Monique Olivier's IQ at 131. Only 3% of the population reaches this figure.

5.
The line of the palm tree

> "Childhood decides."
> Jean-Paul Sartre

April 27, 2014 in Nice

The bell of the parish of Saint-François-de-Paule rang three times. That afternoon, I suggest to Selim to answer Michel Fourniret's mail, so that he confesses his crimes and brings an indication on the location of the pieces of the treasure. I submit various sketches to him. As nothing should be left to chance, I found a hand-picked turquoise postage stamp, which was made by the artist Ben Vautier, and on which is written so beautifully in golden letters: "Words are life. The envelope is ready for mailing.

"So, what do you say?

- I'm a little afraid," Selim replies, turning the page. It would be a lie to say otherwise, it seems to me.

After reading, Selim rejects any conventional use of polite formulas on the letterhead, such as "dad" or even

"Michael", so that there is no ambiguity. Apart from that, I suggest to him to pretend to be in a precarious situation to make him feel guilty. We agree:

Selim, to *Michel Fourniret* - Your reconnection leaves me perplexed, why now? Is fatherly love awakening in prison? Speaking of "media pressure", I have to think about you every day. Outside, in the eyes of everyone, I remain the son of the "ogre of the Ardennes", an infamous pedophile. It's not easy to deal with emotionally. Thank you for the money order, even though I am still very far from making ends meet. I don't have a cross or a battery[5]. May you remember one day that you still got me used to the castle life.

The letter is mailed.

A fortnight later, Selim announced that his father had answered our letter. On May 14, we met again near the Nice Opera House. Selim handed me an unsealed letter with gummed edges, written by Michel Fourniret. Oli," he said, "you will see from this letter that Michel is a complete madman, and that this is a madness without a cure... There is nothing to be learned from it, if you want my opinion. And to add after having finished his cup: "Perhaps we had better abandon this whole story."

Michel Fourniret, *to Selim* - In case your nieces and nephews, offspring of Anne and Jerome, of Wendel and his spouse, of Marvin and his spouse... dream of learning from their uncle Selim, the art of building, from three times nothing = newspaper, and magazines thrown in the trash,

---

5. Being without money.

in full bundles! That is to say three times nothing... added
to a pleasure without name: the pleasure to create, to create
from nothing. Crénom! It is not nothing! Perhaps children
would dream of building, *"launching towards the sun"* the
glider. The aeroplane. Like these planes that pre-war generations taught to make to our post-war generation. Here is
therefore attached to the money order of 400 euros which
you will have the use:

N°1 = Front part (disassembled) of the plane.

N°2 = Tail and wing.

N°3 = Assembly model.

That is to say, enough to found the ecstasy of budding
aviators: the youth of the district. The sector around the
city of Zaïne is going to come alive, metamorphosed that
it risks to be in... aerodrome! It is to a pilot in charge of
the launching of takeoff that it will be up to proceed to the
suitable curvature of the two planes of the back empen-
nage and this, according to *desiderata*. Nose down descent.
Smooth navigation. Before the crash, candle climb so that
the most timid launcher is surprised to cry out: "Hurray!

Such is the wonderful character that Théodore de
Banville portrayed in the pages of what I consider a masterpiece of yesterday's literature. His major work: *Le Clown* ou
Le Saut du tremplin, unforgettable confidentiality between
the clown and his springboard in this memorable passage:

> *When I take a swing, make me*
> *Leap higher, elastic board!*
> *So high that I can't see,*
> *With their cruel black clothes*
> *These grocers and notaries!*
> *Higher still, up to the pure sky! further!*

5. The line of the palm tree

Jules-Louis Gaston Fourniret, your paternal grandfather, an old-fashioned smoker, confided: "I get as much pleasure from rolling it as from smoking it! "Every cent of euro that one does not have to spend, would pontificate Scrooge and other billionaires, helps to bear a little less misery." Every unspent euro enriches the thrifty person with 6.58 new francs. That is to say: an astronomical saving that can be counted in piles of old francs. These precious francs are only thanks to the pennies! Well, well, well! The home-made plane, it's kif-kif! A hundred thousand times more lively than sitting on your ass in front of a small screen. It's up to you, son, to pass it on to your people! Signed, your old man.

***

A paper biplane! It's no wonder that all of this elicits pitying comments such as: "This is unimaginable! Why does this crazy guy encourage me to pick up kids?" asks Selim. It's as if he wants to push me to the fault so that I join him in the ball. Admit it! And that's it! Ah, what a bastard!

Surrounded by mozzarella-colored tourists with their necks whipped by the sun, we spend the rest of the afternoon deciphering the mail and looking for clues about the Postiches' booty.

Before leaving us, Selim pities himself on the "bad tongues of the television", the nose plunged in an umpteenth mug of beer. The evening before, he fell on *Touche pas à mon poste*, the emission animated by Cyril Hanouna, during which a columnist would not have deprived himself of swinging, hilarious: " You would not prefer to be with Fourniret in a cell rather than with Verdez[6] ? He adds other examples straight from a register where a lot of vexations are recorded. This is how I learn that on February 22, 2014, the comedian Jérémy Ferrari answered with a chuckle to a journalist from *Voici* who asked him if it was because he was born in the Ardennes that he developed "this very black humor": "Maybe, yes! Besides, there are quite a few humorists from this region. I think of Rimbaud, Michel Fourniret..." Raising his eyes to the sky, the columnist, joking, continues: "But, you're not afraid of reprisals by always attacking the hottest topics?" Aligning myself with the values of the prince of Sautou - that's the nickname I sometimes give to Selim - and of his sensitive nature, I enter his game: "Here, indeed, a poor joke! As if sketches about a serial killer, already sentenced to life imprisonment, could jeopardize the career of Jérémy Ferrari! By the way, have you ever listened to songs by the rapper Booba?" This conversation leads me to sing a saucy song called *Du biff* in which a certain Mala, in his gravelly voice, threatens reprisals against the Ardennes in the fifth verse: "My group assassinates the Fournirets all in feline thongs, stilettos, lip gloss". All this, clapping his hands in rhythm.

---

6. The journalist Gilles Verdez is a columnist in the show *Touche pas à mon poste*.

At these words, the son of the ogre turns white with fright. Oh, bugger!" he blows, in a clear tone, then answers, always talkative: "It annoys me, but I don't oppose it. Michel has done everything to get there. But if I hadn't had the chance to change my name, well, I would still be bullied. I remember the time when my teachers, at roll call, would ask the Fourniret student to go to the blackboard... What a shame!... My new name? Easier to wear in society than the first one... I am hiding, and yet, I have nothing to reproach myself with. I chose to be innocent. Not having that name anymore is by far the best thing that ever happened to me. Imagine, Oli, how much pain it would have been if a woman and a child had had to bear it... On a symbolic level, it was the best way to deny Mich-Mich, but also to avoid a lynching. Ah! I think of the people in my family who were not so lucky, like my uncle André Fourniret, my many cousins...".

Then, scratching his chin, the ogre's son adds:

"Don't you think the TV clowns could show a little more delicacy?

- Besides, aren't you afraid that the Fourniret case will be brought to the screen one day ? Sooner or later, it will happen.

- Come on! It would be wrong to make us relive this tragedy for pseudo-artistic purposes. It is not appropriate to elevate scum to the status of icon, as was the case for the *Mesrine* saga with Vincent Cassel. What's the point of putting such a monster on top, if not to make money on the back of the dead? This type of film shows, in my opinion, a real lack of sensitivity towards the victims' families. I despise both the authors and the actors.

6.

THE SUPPLICANT OF THE ATLAS

> "It is in the Moroccan Atlas
> that I began to evolve.
> Hervé Gourdel

September 28, 2014 in Vallauris

It is past 1 pm, when Selim points his nose at the foggy horizon. He seems out of his depth. His elocution is laborious. The gray face and the ear broken by the cold, he is not as usual, as attested by his forehead beaded with sweat...
" Hey there! Selim, but you are bleeding! You are hurt..."
Selim's only response then consists of wrapping his gaze around me, while choking on a fresh cut.
"I am seriously considering a career change."
- But, what's wrong with you?"
I'm cursed, you see. I'm cursed for all eternity..." he continues, claiming to have had his leather tanned two days earlier.

***

It is very early that day, when Selim sets out for the Golfe-Juan-Vallauris station. He had to catch the train that would take him to Grasse, to a perfume factory, where he was in charge of security. For information, this former squire lives with the generous André Michaut, the first husband of Monique Olivier. He occupies a dreadful shanty in an old apartment in the Zaïne, a slum of seven masonry towers. This area is landlocked, and is only served by the railroad, to the south, three kilometers away. This asphalt jungle is a real dead end, built on a rocky hillside, accessible by a single road, on the heights of Vallauris, east of Cannes. In short, our friend lives in a rat's nest.

At the edge of the forest where he goes to take his usual shortcut, Selim goes down a winding staircase, under the shade of massive trees. Three paths cross there. He goes up and down the steps, four by four, and has not yet taken a hundred steps when he freezes. Under a bunch of lampposts lies a patrol of young people, dressed in brightly colored shirts. A second quadrille of "Bedouins" appears on the opposite side, increasing the number of the pack from five to seven. Suddenly, they agitate in concert and block his way. Pulling on the straps of his backpack with an astonishing vivacity, his shoulders hunched, his cheeks cracked, the frail man of 1,87 meter tries to make himself very small. So much for his pride. Detecting their intention, he skirts around the band of vagabonds with a swaying step to finally engage in off-trail, thus keeping them at a distance.

"Hey! You! What's wrong with you! What do you want, son of a bitch?..." Selim pretends not to have heard. All the eyes fall on his back, like a rain of arrows, with in premium a string of insults. "Hey, here you are! You dog! Son of a bitch, go! Fuck your grandmother, the queen of the whores! This time, it is the turn of the youngest satyr, jumping like a boxer, to add with a senseless rage: "Oh, yeah? You want to make us a dinguerie, you bastard! With your cowardly body, there..."

Selim, followed by his entourage, responds to the insults by apologizing, eager to avoid any problems that might prevent him from honoring his duties at the factory: "Forgive me. I must go to work." But, nothing to do. These scum are on his heels. With his chin tucked into the hollow of his neck, he continued on his way, bumping into a lamppost, even voluntarily ignoring the clawed hand that was trying to sneak into his bag... Come on, only a few more steps! Too late. In this arrangement, the youngest of them, a dwarf, master of his technique, arms himself with a white stone as sharp as an ice pick, that he had intentionally placed on a concrete ramp, then throws it with all his strength, without any warning.

"Son of a coward!" his assailants chorused. The whistling projectile hits the Fourniret son, planting itself in the back of his neck. At this blow, Selim, whose legs click with each of his strides, utters a heart-rending cry, wavers, and falls. And, while the flag of Japan is drawn slowly on the thick pad of tinder with which he tries to stop the haemorrhage, here is that a second dragée hits him the elbow, carrying with it, on the way, a lock of drusy hairs. A thin net of drool overflows of its twisted mouth, thus going to flower the buttonhole of its parka. "Bastards!", bursts the son of the "ogre of the Ardennes", folded in two, between thousand curses. Selim is already on his feet, steps over the guardrail, and runs away, pursued by the mocking laughter...

"I was attacked for being the symbol of the France that gets up early, me the son of the serial killer, Michel Fourniret. You can imagine!" he exclaims, promising never to use the "Gémonies" staircase again[7] , and to move out as soon as possible. Note that his wrath grows as he tells me about his attack.

To complete his disgrace, when Selim arrives at his workplace, panting with fatigue, his superior, a certain Ricci, has taken the opportunity to lecture him loudly for his tardiness, in full view of all the workers, who are hilarious. In the meantime, Samuel, a co-worker, seeing this, approaches, asking if everything is all right: "Wait, Selim. For God's sake... Selim, your neck!" With a cry of fright, he stands there, pointing a trembling finger at his juicy wound, studded with tiny telluric debris. And there, Selim, reduced to the state of a salt statue in prey to the surf, explains, hardening his voice, as if to feign an assurance that cheers him up: "Oh! You know, Sam, others have lived worse, much worse... Believe me."

***

I am speechless. He is still in shock. He finds only setbacks and heartbreaks by the thousands on his way. Is there nothing more pathetic than our poor friend? What sense can we make of this relentlessness, tinged with incitement to suicide? Hasn't he already suffered enough? In the meantime, Selim announces his imminent departure for Algeria.

---

7. Name of the place where, in ancient Rome, the bodies of the tortured were exposed.

Early in the morning, my visa application was validated," he says, with disconcerting naturalness. I won't be gone very long. I'll be gone for a little over a week, from October 15 to 23. I've just come back from the consulate, you see...

- And what! Algeria, really ? Funny place to hope to have a good time, considering the current events... Come on, my poor fellow, you don't think about it ! Why this choice ?

- By curiosity, of course! retorts Selim, with his usual placidity.

- Who are you going to leave with?

- Nobody. I leave alone to Khenchela, from where I could climb the Saharan Atlas, a rampart that culminates at 2 328 meters, facing the desert.

- Selim! Stop it! My word, you're completely out of order! Why punish yourself like this? None of this is your fault. You don't have to blame yourself. You're free, you know. Even so, you're looking to get yourself cowardly killed by the turbans, like that poor mountain guide, right?"

A week ago, our fellow Frenchman, Hervé Gourdel, was kidnapped in the Djurdjura mountains, near the village of Aït Ouabane, by "soldiers of the caliphate", an Algerian terrorist organization born from a split of AQIM[8], and having pledged allegiance to the terrorist group Islamic State. On September 23, the sentence was carried out: death by beheading, which caused a great stir in the national community, especially on the Mediterranean rim. In the meantime, the terrorists called for the killing, absolutely and indiscriminately, of "an American or European unbeliever - especially the nasty, dirty French."

----

8. Al-Qaeda in the Islamic Maghreb.

That he refuses to use violence to defend himself, by his way of life, is still acceptable... But that he throws himself into the arms of death, at the easternmost extremity of the known world, with the certainty of saving himself from the abyss of despair, is death without a sentence! Will it be necessary to perish to expiate the sins of the Fourniret-Olivier couple? Immediately, I expressed my deep concern, and called on him to cancel his planned trip to Algeria, but he didn't care. On the *other hand,* he proudly compares himself to the eponymous hero of the film *Le voyage de Selim* (1978) by Régina Martial. Set in Châteauroux, one day in November, it recounts the adventures of a young Algerian immigrant in France, charged for a crime he did not commit. "I'm going to shoot the sequel!" he exclaims, laughing. "And, since I'm leaving not far from where Gourdel was kidnapped, I leave you my cell phone. Do we ever know?

- Precisely, Selim! Aren't you afraid to go back to France, head first?

- Not in the least, because the danger is already here, on our doorstep. Yes, it is here," he says, and no doubt with good reason.

Michel Fourniret's son recalls another incident that occurred at Nice-Côte d'Azur airport on August 30, when a 22-year-old Chechen man was arrested by the border police. He was suspected by the intelligence services of recruiting candidates for the holy war, and of having paid in cash for the plane ticket of a sixteen-year-old girl who was about to take a flight to Turkey, with the intention of going to Syria. You see," my friend objects, "the goal of zero risk is just a delusion. We are in danger everywhere. Maybe it's sad, but life has proven to me that you should always expect a serious skirmish, no matter the time or place."

By improvising a great speech, I hoped to bring him back to reason, but since he was stubborn, too bad for him, too bad for me... Two years later, I will be forced to admit that Selim was right... Ultimate strangeness: the prince of Sautou confided to me that he had misplaced his fetish watch, this morning, at the Algerian Consulate. However, he assures me that he has no intention of returning to retrieve it. Why desert? To this other question, he answers: "Time does not exist.

7.

LONG JOHN FOURNIRET

"To the innocent the hands full."

October 26, 2014, in Nice

I didn't see Selim again for a month. No need, however, to think of asking him about his spectacular hike on the slopes of the Saharan Atlas. He doesn't have the slightest desire to talk about it. What did he do that could have attracted this new layer of black clouds? I pretend not to notice anything, so that the tension dissipates by itself.

Selim throws a large brown envelope on the table, eroded on its edges. "There's the mail," he shouts, taking a sip of cappuccino. I realize what this is all about when I see three green postage stamps featuring Marianne, the symbol of the French Republic, whose features were inspired by one of the Ukrainian founders of Femen, Inna Shevchenko. The placement of three "Femen" stamps is the official signature of prisoner number 5451, who never hesitates to waste two extra 20 gram stamps unnecessarily.

I unfold the missive folded in four. It is an indignant letter from Michel Fourniret, rather short.

"What does it tell us?

- Read it instead," Selim replies, with sticky sweat flooding his elongated forehead. "But basically, this jerk is mad that he missed his prank with the paper airplane. He addresses me with authority, like I'm still a kid. Like he's still my dad... but he's just a big, fat, illustrious jerk!"

Now our friend stutters. Then, staring at the old man's padded envelope, he yells in a strangled voice: "Maybe we could have talked about all this face to face, if you hadn't been in prison for beating and savagely raping kids!" In anger, he slams his fist on the table, causing my soda water balloon to sparkle. Three white-collar good guys talking in unison, flinch, giving us a sideways glance.

At first sight, Michel Fourniret seems very angry. After remaining silent for nearly six months, he gets out his claws, irritated by the fact that his correspondent has played the deaf card. It is in this context that he taunts his son Selim, armed with a somewhat perfidious irony:

Michel Fourniret, *to the student Selim* - 1° In four days: one more spring will be added to the twenty-five years of a certain Selim Gwenaël Jean-Pierre. 2° Nothing forbids Selim to suppose that, on this occasion, the thought of an old fool will go towards him. 3° The amount of the expenses of sending a money order by the care of the Post office... exceeding 8 euros - that is to say equivalent to nearly 5 000 old French francs: after the present sending? Quarterly frequency - except in the case of unforeseen events! 4° Your silence is eloquent. Thank you!

***

This reading leaves me perplexed, fearing that I have missed a detail of primary importance. Nothing in this letter justifies such an outburst from Selim. The killer used his usual methods of psychological torture, as in the last minutes of his trial, on May 27, 2008. That day, at the end of the plea of his lawyer, Michel Fourniret had been authorized to speak one last time, and had then extracted from his pocket a paper folded in four on which were written ten devaluing appreciations to the attention of each. His wife, Monique Olivier, was called "a soulless woman who whines like a doormat". The public prosecutor, Francis Nachbar, was reduced to the status of "a rascal, a vituperator, a simpleton on legs". This is not without its piquancy. Besides, I folded the parchment and put it back in its bubble-paper case.

"I exclaimed, after a few seconds of silence. "Is that what's got you in such a state? Because it's not the end of the world!

- You see, it's been eleven years since that bastard scolded me. I didn't know that was still possible. Really, I thought all that was behind me! And here it is again! He treats me like a puppy, shamelessly. He makes me feel guilty for not fulfilling my duties as the son of a pedophile. He wants to regain some of his fatherly authority. But how dare he?"

His heart would drop for a bit, so much he has the shakes.

"My apologies, Dude. This is all my fault. I'm the one who woke the wolf from a deep sleep. But what an idea, too..."

Despite the hindsight he prides himself on, Selim is still as sensitive as ever to his father's poisoned arrows.

"The worst thing is that he must have put a curse on me when he wrote those few lines. I know him, the Mich-

Mich!" Modified by the complementary of the monster, the cheeks of Selim, usually so pale, suddenly turn to vermilion. "You bastard!" he yells. Shearing winds rushed through his cracked armor. As if he was going to fight, here he is rolling up his sleeves, exposing long arms as gaunt as they are hairy, which he relaxes like serpentine whistles.

The odious Michel Fourniret has just manifested here his demiurgic power, beyond the high walls of Ensisheim, where he is incarcerated. Selim! Horror! His entire left forearm is sewn with vile, blistering scars, combined with fresh, jagged cuts that extend to the elbow. At this sight, I suppressed a gagging heart. This is insane... I had never noticed such needlework before. But what is it? What does it mean? Warmed up by so many questions, I bubbled up, then burst, giving in to fear. "What is this thing?", while indicating his scarred arm. "What happened?"

Selim is startled and loses himself in conjectures while crumbling a quignon of bread. I've already told you this story a hundred times," he says nonchalantly. If you don't listen to me, well, that's your problem..." In addition, it should be noted that it sometimes happens to the disinherited prince of Sautou to recriminate when he is summoned to justify himself on a particular fact. Fearing to have offended me, he will finally drop, rolling his eyes: "You see it well, they are scars. At the age of nineteen, I was the victim of a serious car accident due to a stroke. It was on July 10, 2010. After losing control of my motorcycle in the Spaggiari tunnel[9], I ended up in the scenery, that's all."

---

9. Nickname given to the river Paillon in Nice, in reference to the access tunnel dug to carry out the "heist of the century" from the sewers to the safe room of the Société Générale, by Albert Spaggiari and his accomplices in July 1976.

How can it be! His accident was not yesterday. It was five years ago! But the incisions on his arm are fresh, especially since they seem to have been made by human fingernails. What does this motorcycle accident have to do with the scarring on his forearm?

It is on an afternoon similar to this one, that Selim, formerly a food courier, finishes his service in an Italian restaurant on the Cours Saleya, the most animated street in Old Nice. At the end of his shift, around 3pm, after having been mocked by the manager, Selim leaves the restaurant, not satisfied to be done with his day. He straddles his motorcycle, until then firmly attached to a silver ring. It is a little jewel capable of reaching 290 km/h. It is a Honda CB1000 R of 1,000 m3 with a four-cylinder engine and an aluminum chassis. At the time of the facts it is his only property, bought on credit with his meager salary for 12 000 euros.

Once saddled and bridled, Selim puts the gas, direction a crater of asphalt formed under the river of Paillon, in the direction Nice-Italy, and that one commonly calls here the Spaggiari tunnel, in homage to the famous bandit. All of a sudden, Selim doesn't feel like he's part of this world anymore, it's the black hole.

Rapid flashes of light on his iridium visor helmet, in a jerky way, from tubular lamps... These are the last memories of Selim, when he wakes up, mummified, in a hospital room, after having remained unconscious for twenty-four hours. At his bedside, nobody. Not a bumpkin. Fortunately, he came out of it - and it's a miracle that he wasn't killed - with a simple cranial trauma, without fracture. His arm wound had to be stitched. His bright white motorcycle, whose loan he has not yet finished paying off, ended up in the scrapyard, only four months after it was put on the road.

Clinical Information. - Twenty-one year old patient, victim of a road accident on a two-wheeler on July 10, 2010, referred by the intensive care unit of the Saint-Roch hospital on July 14, 2010 for a head injury with loss of consciousness, and an open trauma of the left elbow. The lesion assessment revealed at the cerebral level: *minimal* meningeal hemorrhage, and fracture of the left rock with otorrhagia; at the level of the left upper limb: elbow wound without underlying fracture, without sensitivomotor deficit, nor vascular disorders (sutured in intensive care); multiple dermabrasions.

The patient was transferred from the intensive care unit after 24 hours of induced coma for post-traumatic monitoring. The evolution in the ward was satisfactory. An audiogram was performed on July 22, 2010 as a follow-up to his fractured rock, and revealed mild left conductive hearing loss with normal eardrum.

***

Selim, poor voodoo doll, plaything of an ogre's fury... How many flecks are still hidden under your raven-colored garment... " Mecton, are you sure everything is all right?" I asked, scanning his arm streaked with still fresh lacerations. You know, you can tell me anything. Trust me!" Selim confirms his initial statements, then dissociates himself from them. "All right! Let us say that from time to time, he pleads by giving himself blows of glottis, I feel a sharp sensation of irritation. Then, I scratch the scars, until I tear off the epidermis."

It is obvious that Selim, on whom all the torrents flow in a hurry, has never really emerged from the Spaggiari tunnel.

He remains - despite the passage of time - the emblem of the monstrosity produced by the combined action of his parents. He is the fruit full of bruises that has fallen from a rotten family tree, on which termite mounds are hidden everywhere under the coat of crumbly bark. It is no coincidence that the ogre's son survived this accident. A suicidal person who is convinced to end it all never fails. This is a cry for help, his apparent wounds being a symbol of a bitter struggle for survival.

Calm down," I said. Why don't you tell me when you and Michael last crossed swords?

- He said, his eye rambling, proving that his hearing is indeed impaired.

- The very last time he yelled at you, when was that?

- But let's see!" he exclaims, his face twisted. What a ridiculous idea! He never shouted! Never! Contrary to the image conveyed by the mass media, Selim says, Michel is not as terrifying as he looks. He's naturally quite calm, you know. When we were living under the same roof, he wasn't a man to use bad words or even blaspheme. Oh, no! It would take a minute to tell you what he did to me, because he never abused me. Nothing like that has ever happened to me. That's why I never suspected a quarter of the atrocities that went on behind my back. He was very angry, yes, but as far as I was concerned, the violence never went beyond a simple slap. That said, I can swear that he never, ever, gave me a beating, or even touched a hair on Mother's head, at least in my presence. It's a pity for journalists, but that's how it is! Of course, this doesn't take anything away from the abomination of his crimes... On the other hand, Michel, sensing human beings coming from afar, has the faculty to destroy psychologically without batting an eyelid, by simply using vexing words whispered in the hollow of the ear. With him, violence was latent. It was his way of making a person look bad. In his presence, we were not allowed to laugh, that's all. When he entered a room, he poisoned even the slightest of our joys. We never knew what to do. Depending on the mood of the day, he could react very violently. I repeat, he was violent with his words, but he did not shout. He didn't hit us. He was never violent. We were only subjected to his charisma...

Well," I said, bringing down a heavy hand on her wispy shoulder, before questioning again:

"Do you remember the last time Michel gave you a hard time?"

In answer, his eye sparkles. With a stormy noise, I suddenly disappear under the cheers of the wind, literally sucked into the imaginary kingdom of the prince of Sautou.

8.

A MIRACLE HAPPENS

June 26, 2003

Here we are in the early morning, in a reconstruction of his ash-colored house, topped with a slate roof and built on the edge of a large bewitched fir forest. The sun, filtering through the poorly sanded tile of his room, is pale. "Welcome, Oli, to the family home at 18 rue de Vencimont, on the heights of Sart-Custinne, east of the tip of Givet, in Belgium," comments Selim, who is to serve as my guide. "It's a small, peaceful village of 200 inhabitants, where I feel comfortable," he continues, noting that I am standing here in his bedroom, located on the second floor of the old house, right next to the one occupied by the diabolical alliance. "We've been living here since 1992, when we had to leave the Sautou castle in Donchery. Who knows, if the Breton had not missed his target, let's say it without blushing, how many lives could have been saved!

And Selim, now holding a lighted torch, adds: "Whatever, in Sart-Custinne, I even appreciate the neighborhood, which I hold in high esteem. This shows how pleasant life is here. And for good reason! I don't live in tune with reality yet. I am far too young! I still don't know that my parents are vile pedophiles who swarm with children's corpses along the paths."

No sooner has he finished speaking than a hoarse cry strikes my ear, shattering my peace. I shudder. "It's only Flicka, our dog," he warns me in a distant whisper. Besides, I note that the princely suite, although immense, is only very little furnished. It counts only a bed, a rudimentary desk in oak with a white earthenware inkwell, as well as a large two-leaf wardrobe. No television, or any toys for children here. On a vast shelf fixed to the wall, only an old collection of miniature cars is enthroned.

All of them were given to me by Grandpa Marcel, my maternal grandfather," explains Selim, raising his torch.

- Oh! oh! oh! They are of great value, no doubt?

- Sentimental, for sure!

- And your Grandpa Marcel... Is he still alive?

- I guess so... We are no longer in contact. When the truth came out, Grandpa Marcel preferred to distance himself from me. Is monstrosity hereditary? In his third and last letter, he decided the question by telling me this:

Grandpa Marcel, *to Selim* - In the future, don't write me anymore, don't tell me anything. I'm sorry.

***

With slow steps, I approach the narrow bay window, which overlooks a deep pool filled with brackish water. It's Mich-Mich," says Selim. As a good handyman, he has installed them in each room of the house in order to fully enjoy his large collection of vinyl records, from the phonograph installed in the living room. He loves music. Few know, unfortunately, that he is very much into French variety. Not unhappy to impose his tastes, he is above all someone who needs to feel listened to, more than reason. In the guest room there is also an electric piano, which he got from somewhere. Oh, listen to this, Oli, you'll be really surprised... He often played a few chords on this piano, while trying his hand at vocals. Yes, Mich-Mich loved to sing at the top of his voice! Amazing, isn't it?"

With my ring finger glued to the tile, I highlight on the mist the horizon line of this distant forest that offers itself to my imagination. I listen to it. This is where the "Ogre of the Ardennes" dug tons of small trenches... I read in *L'Est républicain* that he had taken the habit, when he lived in Sart-Custinne, of going to deposit the bodies of his victims in the forest. "The body of Mananya Thumpong, thirteen years old, abducted in Sedan, I read, was found in Belgium, in a fir-tree near Nollevaux. The body of Céline Saison, eighteen years old, disappeared in 2000 in the center of Charleville, in Sugny, still in Belgium. There are countless fantastic theories about this place.

As a child, I didn't have any friends," says Selim. I was quite withdrawn. I guess it's in my nature. For a long time, my only distraction was my bicycle. Often, I went along the big trees planted at the edge of the roads, alone but free...

- Did Monique and Michel let you go out alone, without supervision?

- Yes, you might think that Mich-Mich is so bossy that he won't let me go out, but that's not the case! He doesn't care what happens to me. He's far too busy fixing up this old place...

8. A miracle happens

- To sum up the situation, you could do absolutely anything, but that still gave him the right to yell at you, as soon as he was in a bad mood.

- Without question, yes.

- How about that? Wasn't he ever worried that you might come face to face with a weirdo like him?

- Officially, there is no pedophile, to my knowledge, in Sart-Custinne, at least not until tonight... "

From where I am standing, I can hear the sound of axe blows under the windows. The man from the woods is there, very close. So I am going to witness, if I understand correctly, the last hours of freedom of Michel Fourniret, who will launch himself tonight - and for the last time - into the hunt for virgins, the attempted rape of Marie-Ascension being the final step in his criminal career. Suddenly, my glance is attracted by a geyser of light spouting out of a disemboweled suitcase.

"Selim, where are you going? Are you leaving?

- Yes, today I'm going on a school trip to the Walibi amusement park, which in those days was still called Six Flags Belgium. I'm so excited... For the first time in my life, I'm not going to see the face of that old killjoy anymore. I don't like my dad. Hey, over here! Follow me," he says, motioning for me to follow him. "You'll see, the house is huge!"

Saying this, Selim grabs the handle of his suitcase, and goes to drag it down a long and tortuous staircase with a wooden banister, making it bump roughly against each step. "On the first floor are the kitchen, the living room, a laundry room, a garage, a dining room, and Michel's workshop," the guide says, noting that this is the largest room in the spacious building with its mansard roof and dormer windows. "What does it hide? Ha! ha! ha! No less than two attics!" Through a string of rooms, Selim leads me over chests, vases, and unsteady piles of gold piastres scattered in profusion here and there on a hand-knotted carpet. "There has always been a lot of money in the house," says Selim, who immediately invites me to take a seat on the sofa in the living room, with its low ceiling and walls covered entirely in red bricks. There, in front of the lit stove, the specter of Monique Olivier vegetates, hands clasped, in front of the television, plunged in a deep mutism. "Mother" loves to watch *Julie Lescaut*, her favorite series! "Mich-Mich, him, it is rather *Inspector Derrick*."

Immediately, a question pops up in my mind: all these stupid police series, would they have served, in spite of themselves, to inculcate pedagogical virtues necessary to Monique Olivier and Michel Fourniret in the active learning of crime scene make-up? And then, they named their dog Flicka, isn't that funny? Suddenly, Selim changes his face, and warns me:

"Oli, he might pop up any minute for me.

- Who is it? The ogre?"

Outside, the axe blows intensify. To all this, join great bursts of voices. "Bad! Bad-bad! Bad-bad!" In the incartade, I hardly dare to breathe, for fear of seeing Michel Fourniret disembark, his arm armed with a burning poker, quick to search our entrails. "Bad! Bad, bad, bad! Bad!", he cries out, through the sky, in front of the door of this old stone building. His voice is strong and low. It seems to get closer as it gains momentum, and as the gingerbread bricks of this house unravel in the increasingly unbreathable air. It remains to learn the reasons for the anger of the "ogre of the Ardennes"...

I purposely omitted to tell you a detail," Selim confessed, lowering his broad forehead. Let us say that I am not what one can call an arrow...

- But still?" I retorted, with effort, filling my pockets with precious stones and imaginary gold coins, all adorned with a laurel branch, and engraved with the coat of arms of Mexico, representing a royal eagle perched on a prickly pear tree, devouring a snake.

- I'm just a damn dunce who didn't get any kind of education, that's all! On the other hand, my brothers and sisters have had a brilliant academic career. For example, Jean-Christophe has the noble profession of radiology manipulator. Anne is an engineer. I'm a security guard... Ah, that's a big deal... Michel has letters. He speaks like a book. For many of us, he could even have become Prime Minister of Belgium if he had wanted to, which is far from being my case... Ah that!

- Okay, but why are you telling me all this now?

- Bad! Bad, bad, bad! Bad, bad, bad, bad, bad, bad, bad, bad, bad, bad, bad, bad, bad, bad, bad, bad, bad, bad, bad, bad, bad, bad, bad, bad, bad, bad, bad, bad, bad, bad, bad, bad, bad, bad, bad, bad, bad, bad, bad, bad, bad!

- Selim!" I grumbled, suddenly seized with a mad terror, my pockets stuffed with gold to sink to the bottom of a lake. "What's all this racket? Are you going to tell me what's going on, or what the hell?

- Michel just found my quarterly transcript in the mailbox," he announced, taking a few steps back. "He's half mad with rage. He's ashamed of me, and he's going to show up soon on purpose. From there, we're off on a chain of events that will lead to drama."

Boom! A moment later, the locks and the hinges of the front door give way to the efforts of the forester of the

Ardennes, coming down to the ground in a great din. For reasons that escape me, the details of his torn face evade my senses. He has no face. The bulb bursts. I cannot see anything, this time. Nothing, except a confused reflection on a pair of glasses behind which sparkle black cavities, deep, struck by flashes of blue light. "Bad! Bad-bad! Bad!". In front of this drawbridge, then, he appears to me, materialized in the form of a vast mass of black and smoky fog, with the acrid breath. Little by little, he slips on the landing, puts his foot on a log, and rushes on his prey, Selim, whose long ears he shreds with his dunce's cap, making his sempiternal joust fall on him: "Bad! Bad-bad! Bad-bad!"

In prey to the *furor*[10], the ogre raises with both hands, above our heads, his school desk, whose inkwell runs out with slow jerks on the ground. In a very strange way, the liquid which escapes from it is reduced at once in a choking vapor. To finish, he goes to throw it on board his white Citroën C 25 van, under the pretext of wanting to sell it at the flea market of Ciney, "to whoever will make a better use of it". Immediately, the brakes screech, the tires squeal. And everything becomes black again.

***

We are back in the present, empty-handed. "It's raining cats and dogs in the backyard of the Wobben," Selim says, with deep bitterness. After having phagocyted this rich legacy of memories, I choose to take over from him, from my few readings in the "miscellaneous" section. "Let's see if

---

10. In Latin, the *furiosus* is the one whose insanity makes him dangerous for his life as well as for the life of others. It is the being reached of murderous madness, the furious madman whose state is made of temporary crises.

8. A miracle happens

I know my Fourniret inside out. If it is so, this day, I launch me, your father will launch out one last time in search of the myth of the virginity, by trying to rape a certain Marie-Ascension, thirteen years old, the one who will allow his capture, isn't it?" Selim says "yes" with his head.

On Thursday, June 26, 2003, around 2 p.m., a young girl with a tanned complexion named Marie-Ascension left the family home in Ciney, where her parents, both of Burundian origin, had come to live a few years ago. The Republic of Burundi is a purely continental country in East Africa, without any access to the sea. There is no way out in Wallonia either... Invited to a birthday party, the teenager goes to the supermarket near the train station, only three hundred meters from her home, with the sole purpose of buying a greeting card. Poor thing! She barely had time to take three steps when a Citroën C 25 stopped at her level and accosted her. Michel Fourniret rolled down the window and asked her, pretending to be in a hurry: "I have to go to Mont-de-la-Salle. Can you show me the way? I'm not quite sure I understand. In these woods, all the roads look the same. Get in! You're going to guide me." For the record, Mont-de-la-Salle is a training center of a Catholic religious organization called Maison provinciale des frères des écoles chrétiennes de Belgique francophone. With a weary gesture, a clear indication of her good education, Marie-Ascension declined the invitation.

"I can't get into strangers' cars.

- Well, well! Bravo!" exclaimed the ogre. You are right, my child. Every day, I tell my son Selim the same thing. Besides, you must be the same age as him. Say, you look very big for your age. Come on, don't be afraid! I have children, I'm an art teacher", the forester from the Ardennes carefully insists in an enveloping voice, fatally betraying his tyrannical paternalist power. Then wagging his index finger, incensed, in a falsely professorial tone: "It's not good not to trust people. That's how the world goes wrong!"

He opens the door on the passenger side. In front of so much gouaille, the innocent Marie-Ascension bends her back, and ends up taking place at the front of the vehicle. As soon as she got in, the van sped off in the direction of Dinant, away from the crowd, making the dust fly on the side of the road. Not fooled, the little girl asked to get out. At these words, the tone hardens.

"Shut up, or I'll hit you!" warns Michel Fourniret, threatening her with the edge of his hand, before hammering her with questions: "Are your parents poor or rich? What is your name? Are you a virgin?

- Don't hurt me!" retorted Mary Ascension, before adding: "Do you believe in God? If you believed in God, you wouldn't be doing what you're doing!"

Speaking like this, Marie-Ascension took refuge in prayer. "Hail Mary," the pious teenager said out loud, without suspecting the significance of this phrase, which had far-reaching consequences. "Hail Mary, full of grace. The Lord is with you. You are blessed among all women and Jesus, the fruit of your womb, is blessed. Holy Mary, Mother of God, pray for us poor sinners, now and at the hour of our death. Amen."

The prayer of Ave Maria is welcomed by a black look, but so be it! Marie-Ascension will repeat it three times, in spite of the summons to keep quiet which is made to her by the "ogre of the Ardennes", whose reason has just fallen in distaff. Then, he gives a brutal brake, rushes savagely on the small girl zealous for the religion, throws her on a blue tarpaulin on which rests the office of Selim, in the back of the vehicle. With the help of a leather strap, he binds her feet with a cord that he connects directly to the already tied wrists, the whole being directly attached to the body pillar. "You are of the band with Dutroux?", asks the girl. It is at this precise moment that Michel Fourniret pronounces this sentence which says a lot about his imminent intentions: "Me, I am worse than Dutroux!"

231 kilometers from Ciney, a miracle occurs in an unexplained way. Marie-Ascension managed to free herself from the canvas and, taking advantage of a stop at a crossroads, escaped from the vehicle, and left, hopping, to hide in a corn field nearby. She was quickly taken in charge by a kind-hearted person named Stéphanie Janton to whom she shared her misadventure. Aware of the drama that has just unfolded, she takes Marie-Ascension on board, and takes the pedophile on the hunt in the hope of getting his license plate number. The scenario envisaged occurs. Second miracle : on the way, the white van resurfaces, coming from the distant horizon. Marie Assomption confirms that it is indeed the man who tried to kidnap her. Stéphanie Janton then memorizes the license plate, and they all rush to the nearest police station. According to the police, the vehicle belongs to Monique Olivier, until then unknown to the police. An hour later, Michel Fourniret is stuffed into the salad basket, as soon as he returns home. He offered no resistance. After the first interrogation, he was transferred to the Dinant prison, charged with kidnapping, indecent assault on a minor, and then imprisoned. It is in this context that the Fourniret case begins, each day bringing its batch of abominable crimes, covering a period from 1987 to 2003.

***

And then, when the time came to explain himself to the investigators," says Selim, with a very strong emotion in his voice, "this asshole had the nerve to say that it was all my fault, because I had brought him a bad report card, which had put him in a memorable rage. As if that was enough to justify an attempted rape... Can you imagine? Marie-Ascension was thirteen, and I was fourteen. We have only one year of difference. I turned twenty-seven, last September 9. In a perfect world, she and I could have been friends. Who ever saw so many vices united in one man? How lowly!"

Raising a palm to Selim, I greet this calculation with deep indignation. "Go!" I say, a little stunned by his tale. Stop lamenting! I am not a man to consider that it is whining that will make you advance. Enough of this!

- It's true," Selim replies. That's right."

Eleven years have passed since that famous summer morning in 2003. In the long run, Selim has internalized his anger and has never told his four truths to this rabid father who has taken so much of his life, having gone so far as to commit the insult of making him responsible for his most vile impulses, he who has depopulated the Belgian and French regions for so long. According to me, Selim, if he thinks of saving his soul, must take revenge on him. It must be the same for Michel Fourniret, and even more so for everything that belongs to him. It must be the logical continuation. Without doubt, it is high time to give him back the blows one by one, without taking any chances, so that the Prince of Sautou can be afloat, otherwise I am afraid he will lose his mind.

O "Ogre of the Ardennes"! Your own son and I will trample your sick brain. You glory in being "worse than Dutroux"? We are ready to avenge a thousand injustices in this regard, and to strip you of your boyars[11]! Selim bends over the envelope of prisoner no. 5154, charging it with imprecations as if his father were here, among us:

"I'm sick and tired of my taxes being used to pay for your room and board. We should kill them all, those pedophiles, rather than paying them a hotel for life. Huh! More seriously, why don't you kill yourself in your thebaid, on top of the most beautiful gallows, you fucking bastard? Huh!?" says Selim.

- That is quite true and, I must say, quite deserved," I added, presenting him with a nice bowl of cider. "He'll pay us for this! Unfortunately, the answer is no, no, and a thousand times no! It is still too early, much too early.

- Too early? Selim repeats regretfully, bringing a drained cup to his lips.

- In a manner of speaking.

- But, too soon to do what?"

This time, we enter straight into the heart of the matter. Seeing the prince of Sautou so prodigiously reduced to lint, I take my breath, and say to him:

"My dear Selim, would you like to venture with me on the trail of the sunken treasure of the Postiches?"

"Hey what! No ? You don't want to?", I inquired after a few minutes, looking dazed, and with both eyebrows cocked. "No way!

---

11. Fictitious money to be collected by the adventurers of the game show of France 2, *Fort Boyard*.

- Uh! Uh! Uh!" he exclaims at the end. Would I like that? Ah! Ah! I even demand it. I would be delighted to help. It would be the crowning achievement of my life. Only... What must be done?

- Nothing could be easier, comrade! I'm signing you up as the Kyann Project scribe right now. You will do exactly as I say, no questions asked. You must confide in me. That's the way it is. Only, let's keep it between us! In school, you were good at dictation and writing, despite your poor results in other subjects?

- Respect for spelling is my only quality," he exclaims, with decorum, in a voice that is becoming increasingly greedy.

- That's great! So I've come to ask you a favor. A favor in exchange for which, if you agree, I will give you what you need. I expect you to devote all your efforts to writing to the ogre under my dictation. I am the one pulling the strings. But my name and signature must never appear, for obvious reasons.

- Period ?

- Period, and you will be rewarded...

Good! Good!"

Then Selim reaches into his pocket and pulls out a dealer's card from under the folds of his coat, which he holds out to me, stretching his arm over a brown puddle of caffeine. "I want to be able to ride a nag, but not just any nag: the KTM 690 SMC R super bike, that's my condition. To buy this jewel, I need 15,000 euros, if you know what I mean... Not to mention the fact that I still have to pay back 9,000 euros to my bank. Are you there yet? Are you there?"

In other words, the disinherited prince of Sautou suggests, with prodigious volubility, the granting of a planned gift in cash.

8. A miracle happens

"Well! Count on me to pass your list on to Santa. You're not alone now.

- Hey! Hey! It's a deal! I'll do it, and all the other things that will be useful to the families of the victims who are still waiting for Mich-Mich to regain the use of speech.

- In this case, there is not a minute to lose! Let's lard the bastard, let's fish him out properly! We have to."

And now, let's get to work. *In cauda venenum.* Any text that takes advantage of it must first flatter its interlocutor and this, with the only and unique goal to stun him in order to better shoot him down. Here is the letter that we write:

Selim, *to the student Fourniret* - I have been very busy. I work a lot. To earn my living, I hold several jobs. At the same time, what's the point of writing to you if you don't bother to answer my questions properly? Stop talking. You're always beating around the bush. In the future, try to be more clear! And please, stop playing Don Quixote! Watch out for the irrelevance!

1°) What is the point of contacting me again, ten years later?

2°) Do you love me as a father should love his son?

3) Why don't you ever ask how I am? Can it be that you miss me sometimes?

4°) Why do you always refer to the Holy Trinity? What does it hide?

5°) Do you feel regret for what you have done to the families of the victims, without forgetting your own?

6°) I would like to know the whole story from the beginning. I only know the mass media version. Now I want to know yours. I hear you are writing a book. I would appreciate it if you would share it with me. Maybe it will help me understand you better, who knows?

7°) And mom?

8°) I often have this same dream. I would like you to explain it to me. I'm walking, lost in the dark forest of Clairefontaine-en-Yvelines. I have one foot stuck in the grave, between the rue de Paincourt, and the impasse des Maisons-Blanches. Explain to me such a nightmare, when I have never been there, or at least, not in my memories...

9°) Since you've been behind the high walls of Ensisheim prison, you've let your beard grow. Who is hiding behind this hairpiece?

It's signed Rémi, as *Rémi sans famille*[12].

***

"Soon, very soon, you and me, we will dig up this damn hoard", says Selim, while licking in turn the nipples of the pretty Femen, offering herself to him on the virgin envelope. "After that, Oli, we'll sail to Zihuatanejo with a good breeze[13]. There, we will sip Ti'punch at will on a beach, in resort clothes, in a house on stilts." Getting up to run away from the Wobben, I said to him out of pure compassion, "Ah, by the way, happy birthday, comrade!"

---

12. *Rémi sans famille is* a Japanese cartoon broadcast in 1977, adapted from the novel *Sans famille* by the French writer Hector Malot.
13. Zihuatanejo is a city in the state of Guerrero, Mexico. Reference to the film *The Escaped* (1994) by Frank Darabont, based on the novel *Rita Hayworth and the Shawshank Redemption* by Stephen King.

9.
PROMETHEUS IN CHAINS

"Man is a god in ruins."
Ralph Waldo Emerson

Monday, November 3, 2014, in Nice

On the eve of my departure for the free city of Christiania, Denmark, a sheet of parchment arrived addressed to the ogre's son: "No answer is given. It was all talk, nothing but talk. In spite of that, we pressed where it hurts! His armor is dented and cracked everywhere... Storm warning." See how promptly Michel Fourniret applied himself to answer us. "He is known for his art of making himself wanted", the magistrates and police officers of the Crim' would rightly tell you.

Once entrenched in the estaminet, I find Selim, all sighing. He starts to mimic the powerful sword blow with the murderous point that he has just made to his father, and this, in spite of the distance that separates them. "And paf!", he cries, the glance full of malice, before pushing a rattle of contentment. I imagine Michel Fourniret jumping on his spring bed.

Michel Fourniret, *to Selim* - When I got back from the shower, as soon as I read your letter received at the end of the morning, a letter that I will echo later, once my furious desire to pounce has passed! Fucking assholes to the power of ten! What? Your old man, writing a book? Assertion worthy of oxen which, passive, would become creators, without their hair in the pogne which vows them to the statute of spectator, of undead, half-brancher, half-idolater of the god Television.

Fucking assholes to the power of ten! Why would I write a book, when dozens are swarming in my head? When, piled up for years, over the years, full bundles of first drafts are maturing, among which *Le Faubourg des enclos*. The setting: paradise. Here, Satanius and Fahivinius, sworn enemies, are buddies like pigs. In fruit growing, the apple tree is the tree that bears apples. Pear tree? The tree that bears pears, and cherry? The tree that, in season, gives up to our greed, its sour cherries that it has long, long ripened ... The *Jetaimier*? Tree which, to this unknown day, makes it cover itself with *I love you*? Mystery and gumdrop!

As for offering you my interpretation of this singular dream that takes advantage of your sleep to transport you to Clairefontaine-en-Yvelines? Something to be puzzled about, really puzzled. Quite moved, too... An invitation to the initiative of Mother Nature who never says, never does anything without reason... She! Go figure! I suggest you talk to Anne, your big sister. Stop.

***

As I finish these words, a drop of icy water finds its way into the neckline of my shirt. The grayish sky has swollen with clouds full of melancholy, which are now crying over the city, which precipitates our departure under a covered terrace. We settle down near a table occupied by two affable Belgians with a delicious Liège accent:

"I exclaimed, nudging Selim with my elbow, but he was reluctant.

No!" he growls, intractable.

- Is that so? Why is that?

- Forget it, will you?

- Well, come on, I insisted. It would be really too stupid. You always complain about being single. You lived in Belgium for a long time. That's a good argument to start a conversation. Ask them if we can sit with them.

Selim cuts to the quick, terse. "No, no and no!" There is nothing to be done. He opposes a fierce resistance to the prospect of a round table. Then his eyes darken, go astray, and his voice hardens, which in my opinion indicates the cursed part of his heritage. "But, what happens, in the end?" The son of the ogre tucks his neck into his shoulders, exasperated at the idea of having to justify himself, clasping his hands together as if in prayer, then whispers to me, tremolos in his throat: "I refuse to let them hear us discuss Sart-Custinne, and the Ensisheim prison. They certainly know about the case... But I refuse to let them know! Who knows, these girls may have friends, or even relatives, who were hurt by my father. We don't know. But why is it so difficult to understand this?

What the little prince of Sautou says is full of reason. After a short silence, I nod, resigned, in the hope of obli-

9. Prometheus in chains

ging him to repress the anger which is developing in him. A little later, a light smile finally appears on his lips. Phew! Now, I know. Although he has long since rebuilt his life under a new identity, he is still in the grip of a traumatic internal overflow. We have concluded once again that Michel Fourniret needs to undergo a new shock therapy.

This letter to the ogre will be placed under the sign of one of the great Greek myths which transcends it, that of the chained Prometheus. For having given fire to men, this Titan was condemned by Zeus to be tied to a column and to have his liver eternally nibbled by an eagle.

Selim, *to Michel Fourniret* - "Blessed is he who has been able to penetrate the secret causes of things", said Virgil. You might have thought that this quote was tailor-made for you. But *no, it's* not! It's not for you, as the willy willy has the pretention of believing himself, like Nelson *Mandeila*, "the captain of your soul". Unlike you, he did not kill anyone. On the contrary! It was his own revolutionary ideas that both condemned him and got him out of prison. You, the "ogre of the Ardennes", are only the eternal slave of those innocent little girls on whom you cowardly raised the sword, those whom you caused to perish in the spring of their lives.

No other future civilization will legitimize such actions. So you will never be immortal like the academics, despite your fondest wish. As Auguste Comte rightly said: "The dead govern the living". Submit to the authority of the latter. Living or not, you will remain forever stuck where you already are, behind the bars of a cell, alone, totally unable to create. Like Prometheus, you are condemned to let your liver be devoured every day by a vulture with hair like a cherub.

P.S.: In accordance with your wish, I will write to my older sister, Anne.

With a look inflamed with revenge, the bird-child throws him: "Prometheus me to be nice in Ensisheim!"

"Give me back my Postiche!", retorts the Ardennes, suddenly agitated by spasms, because panicked at the idea of having his liver tingled for the whole eternity.

Holding my pen without pity, I pierce with red ink a vast flap of its right flank. An arrow linked to the bird of ill omen, in front of the number 5451, presents this inscription in bloody letters: "Isabelle, Fabienne, Jeanne-Marie, Élisabeth, Natacha, Céline, Manaya, and how many others? At the foot of the commemorative inscription of Michel Fourniret's "known" victims, I draw one of those toys that children love: a wooden cube marked with letters of the alphabet, with a new coded message on each side: X, O, K. "X" for the treasure, and "O.K." for "I accept this mission". Sometimes a little drawing is better than a long speech.

***

The next day, just before Selim started his shift as a night watchman in a palace on the Monegasque coast, I showed him my sketchbook. Do you recognize this person?" I asked, presenting him with the Fourniret chained to his crimes, eager to know his opinion.

"What a humiliation!" exclaims Selim, hiding his laughter behind a hairy paluche. "Ha! Ha! Ha! For sure, you've outdone yourself! It is very similar. In despair, he will break his head against the walls of his dungeon. He is a dominator. He'll never stand the thought of being thrown in irons to be used as fodder for a little lisp, no matter how cute he is!"

Once Selim has copied the letter, I slip it into an envelope sealed with a stamp with a prophetic meaning, proclaiming in large letters: "Let's recycle our waste".

***

On November 21, 2014, the answer materialized in the form of an offering, in this case a compilation including the seven adventures in comic book form of Luc Junior, a young reporter created by Goscinny and Uderzo. But how did the prisoner get this brand new album, which I didn't even know existed? And first of all, what for? I don't believe, indeed, that Selim is fond of comics. No really, I don't believe it. But then, what is the use? I open the book in the middle, leaf through it... Here! There is a yellow bookmark on page 33, right at the beginning of the chapter entitled... Oh! dog... I can't believe it! I'm stunned. Michel Fourniret decoded very well the message that Selim and I threw at him in order to facilitate the adoption of a common language, so I don't understand it anymore. The chapter of *Luc Junior that* he wants to draw special attention to is entitled, hang on to it, "The Stolen Jewels", which, in other words, means that he agrees to help Selim.

***

Excited by the way things were going, the Prince du Sautou immediately applied for a visit permit to the central prison in Ensisheim. In his letter to the director, a man named Michel Schwindenhammer, I submit to the Prince du Sautou the idea of passing ourselves off as a small homosexual couple, which would give us, for sure, a sort of immunity against any risk of rejection. Because finally, if the penitentiary staff discovers that I am a journalist, we are cooked. Selim declines the proposal.

Selim, *to Michel Schwindenhammer* - Mr. Director, I hereby request a visit permit for inmate number 5451, also known as Michel Fourniret. I am his son Selim. You will find enclosed all the documents that attest to my parentage. At the same time, I would like to inform you of my wish to obtain an extension, going beyond one hour and a half. Please accept, Mr. Director, the expression of my best feelings.

P.S.: I also ask that you grant the request of my friend, Oli Porri Santoro. Visiting my father in his care will, I know, make this time much easier for me.

***

I, *to Michel Schwindenhammer* - Mr. Director, by the present letter, I ask you the right to be able to visit, with my friend Selim, the prisoner Michel Fourniret, whose prison number is 5451. Not being a relative, but rather a close friend of his son Selim, I beg you, at his request, to grant me permission to accompany him, in order to support him in this difficult ordeal. I am a moral support for him. He has not faced his father for more than ten years now. Thank you in advance for your understanding. I look forward to your reply. Please accept, Mr. Director, the expression of my sincere greetings.

***

A week later, our request was endorsed by a letter of support from the prison administration.

***

Michel Schwindenhammer, *to Selim and me* - Gentlemen, in response to your request for the issuance of a visitation permit for Mr. Michel Fourniret, currently incarcerated at the Ensisheim central prison, please take note of the following information:

Your visit permit has been issued by the Director of the facility on a permanent basis. Yours sincerely

***

I invite Selim to follow to the letter the instructions left by the "ogre of the Ardennes" by writing to his older sister, Anne, whom he has not seen for ten years. Let's do it, even if it means obeying him like a bat out of hell. There must be a reason why Michel Fourniret is so insistent that Selim re-establish a dialogue with her. Moreover, I learn that the address of the impasse des Maisons-Blanches, in Clairefontaine-en-Yvelines, often quoted by our good man, was previously his. Who knows? Perhaps Anne is in possession of key elements...

Selim, *to Anne* - You will be surprised by the unexpected nature of this letter. First of all, how are you? And your family? I don't hide from you that I am disappointed not to have heard from you throughout this last decade. I, for one, am making do. However, if I write to you, it is also and especially to know why our father insists so much that

I write to you... What do you know? And you, are you in contact with him ? Tell me everything. Take care of yourself.

I am still your brother Selim, whether you like it or not.

***

His answer will not be long in coming. On December 4, 2014, Selim, whom I pass on the outskirts of L'Almira Wobben, hands me an already opened envelope.

Anne, *to Selim* - Hello little brother, I was indeed surprised to receive your letter, I did not expect it. It arrived on my birthday. It is a beautiful gift, and I thank you for it. Contrary to what you seem to think, I tried to contact you at the last address I found when Marie-Hélène died. A home in the south of France. They wouldn't give me your contact information, so I left them mine to give to you.

I then heard from André, with whom I am in contact. He had told me that you were living at André Michaut's house. Without any news from you, I didn't try to reach you, thinking that you were well there. And then life goes by... very quickly. I am the mother of a little girl and a little boy who occupy and fill a good part of my life with Jerome, whom you have already met. I have also distanced myself from the "business". I have kept myself from it... I have finally almost forgotten it.

Today, Michel Fourniret, whom I call "the other", seems to want to bring us together. I don't need him to want to see you again, to know how you are, so that you and I are no longer alone, survivors of a very sad story. I am lucky to still have my mom with whom I am very united, but what do you have?

The "other" has no contact with me, and that's better. I think bitterly that he only knows how to destroy everything he touches. There was a time in my life when I thought I existed in his eyes, but I doubt it now. Your letter opens me today to other perspectives, than those of an extinguished past, a past that is missing somewhere, which was not so bad. You are welcome here. I think we have a lot to talk about. Could we meet again soon? Can you call me so we can arrange it? See you soon, love you. Your sister, Anne.

***

Being satisfied with his sister's explanations, Selim - who usually has three times the bad luck - now says he is thinking about going to spend Christmas at her place, in the Paris suburbs.

During our first meeting, he had twice confided in me his deep suffering on this subject, convinced that he had been disowned by everyone: "Christmas? It's hard. At home, André and my brothers refuse to celebrate Christmas. The last time I celebrated it, I was fourteen years old. That's right! Anne is married and has two children. No one wants to deal with the spawn of the evil alliance. Because you understand, I may carry within me the seeds of violence, pedophilia and sadomasochism... Which makes me a Proust's madeleine leaving a bitter, if not putrid taste in the gullet..."

As for Michel Fourniret, offended to have been drawn in such a ridiculous outfit and situation, he tore our letter into a thousand pieces, which he then mended with scotch tape - as if he regretted his impulsiveness - and then sent it back to the sender.

10.

ANDRE THE MAGUS

"O Simon the Magician!
O wretches who follow in his footsteps!
You whose rapacity prostitutes,
for gold and for silver,
the things of God, brides for the good;
it is appropriate that for all sounds
now the trumpet."
Dante

December 8, 2014 in Paris

It is about 5 a.m. when a violent vibration is felt under the pillow. "You'll never guess, Oli, what I've come to tell you. At the other end of the line, my friend Selim wakes me up from my sleep, repeating the same sentence with a serious air: "He is here! An enemy power has entered his field of vision. It's about the Postiches gang, you know, that Bellaïche," he murmured. Imagine that he has just burst into the supermarket where I provide security, in Antibes."

At these words, I froze.

- "But what are you singing to me? Have you been drinking?

- Never on my shift, of course.

- But then, this Bellaïche... Is he the one who... How is he?

- You tell me, that's what I'm calling about...

- Don't leave Selim for a moment!"

Bellaïche!" I exclaimed, rushing out of bed towards my modest library. I then flipped through the yellowed pages of the breviary of crime history:

André Bellaïche was the leader of the Postiches gang, a team of mythical robbers who were champions of disguise, but he never admitted it. He was never convicted of the 27 robberies that plagued France from September 1981 to January 1986, and always denied being part of the gang [...] Their bloody epic, in which some of them had already lost their lives, came to an end on January 14, 1986, with the attack on the branch of the Crédit Lyonnais on rue du Docteur-Blanche in Paris (16th district). A policeman was shot and Beau Sourire was also killed. Twelve months later to the day, the police "jumped" the rest of the gang in a house in Yerres (Essonne). In 1996, the Court of Assizes rendered its verdict: Marguery and Myszka were sentenced to twelve years in prison. The latter committed suicide in 2003 after a long psychiatric wandering. André Bellaïche, now free, will only get eight years. His colleague Marguery, also free, went to live in Asia. Patrick Geay, arrested in 2004, was sentenced to 17 years in 2006. He is still incarcerated to this day.

Now that's strange. I imagine the chilling scene at the supermarket security checkpoint, featuring a shadowy figure draped in a mastic raincoat, facing the serial killer's son:

"Good evening sir, to whom do I have the honor?

- Me? It's Bellaïche", he will say, in a hoarse voice. "You got the Postiches' hello!"

Selim explains to me that the individual in question is still present in the premises.

"Now tell me," I cried, turning pale, "are you in danger?

- Oli, we won't argue any longer. Come and find me at the Almira Wobben for 8 o'clock. Good night!"

I show up at the Wobben, a good hour late, which has the gift of annoying him. Without saying a kind word, Selim grabs a fold straight out of his bag, slides it on the table to the edge, nodding his chin, just before planting his fangs in a delicious crescent moon, shooting stars in his eyes.

I turn the document over, and discover a black and white photocopy of an identity card attributed to a certain Lilah Bellaïche.

It's funny to note that this character seems to have escaped straight from *Looney Tunes*. Up close, he resembles - not without a certain irony - that dear Vil Coyote. His jet eyes are like 12-pound cannonballs ready to be lit. Given the events of last night, I conclude that this must be the individual who broke into his workplace. Obviously, it was not the Postiches' supreme leader, but that doesn't solve the problem, since they both share the same last name.

André Bellaïche must be at least sixty-five years old, while our suspect is thirty-five. With a face like that, I want to believe that Lilah is capable of hiding two or three sticks of dynamite, but from there to say that he has taken over from the Postiches, there is a world! However, it would not be astonishing if a descendant of the gang, deprived of his succession, had concurred to disturb the ordinary hours to recover his property by piercing the side of the geocoucou, in other words the Bip-Bip of Charleville-Mézières. That would even seem rather logical to me... Imagine the reaction of the Postiches when they discovered that they had been plucked...

I am surprised that no journalist has bothered to interview André Bellaïche about the Fourniret case... This is very strange, especially since the other highlight of this sad spectacle is poor Jean-Claude Myszka who, tired of having searched for his treasure in vain since his release in 1999, took his own life at his mother's house on February 11, 2003, without knowing the background of the events. Through the fault of one man, the life of the Postiches was shattered. This man is Michel Fourniret. It is him, and nobody else, who is at the origin of his suicide.

Three decades later, the affront has never been washed away. The man with the cold look on the official document is not just a namesake of the Belleville gang leader. Lilah Bellaïche was also born in Paris, where he still lives, judging by what is written on the back of his identity card. So what was he up to in Antibes in the middle of the night? Was it a warning shot? But, how would he have managed to know the new identity of the offspring of the diabolical alliance?

Last night, Selim explains, he was in charge of stocking the shelves in the store as part of a small temporary assignment. Since access to the store is strictly subject to the issuance of a badge, the loan of the badge required the deposit of a pledge in return, an ID for example. It was his choice to leave his ID card with me. It felt funny to read his name on it when he handed it to me. As soon as he turned his back, I made a photocopy. And that was it!"

Notwithstanding his sleepwalking appearance, Selim showed great foresight. He sensed that something was wrong, and he reacted accordingly.

"Well! Could it be that Lilah is in cahoots with you know who?" asks Selim.

- There's only one way to find out," I retorted, getting up from the table.

Back home, I open a preliminary investigation on this handler in order to make sure of the accuracy of his filiation. Alas, there is indeed a mix-up. At the end of a quick examination, I discover that Lilah Bellaïche lied about his status as a small convenience store employee, since judging by the legal information published in the trade and company register, he would be a company manager in the textile industry. He would own no less than two clothing stores. One in the capital, the other in Saint-Tropez. What interest for him to accomplish dirty jobs to earn three times nothing? In full knowledge of the facts, can't we see the proof that Lilah Coyote is acting undercover with the sole purpose of approaching Selim? Is André Bellaïche the main instigator of a probable punitive expedition?

What to do? Protect him by the fool that I am? To remain motionless? I take the resolution to go to the capital, in the hope of finding André Bellaïche, and to ask him for an interview, taking the pretext of wanting to get his autobiography, *My Life Without a Hairpiece*, published in 2007, and from which the film *The Last Gang* is directly drawn. It is my duty to ward off any evil directed against my friend.

According to comments provided by the press, the latter would have "re-entered" the record business. He would sell his junk in his three stores in Belleville, Abbesses and rue Mouffetard, in Paris. You wouldn't think of selling records like that in the age of illegal downloading! At the time of the restocking of the shelves, it is specified in a report that it is not rare to cross him on his scooter, on which a whole load of DVD is piled up in totem.

So I call the record store on rue Mouffetard directly. There was a long silence on the other end of the line, but a soft, slow voice finally told me: "André is there every night from 10pm to midnight. You can't miss him."

I take care to inform Selim of my departure for the City of Light on board a train, all this in the only purpose to avoid him an armed conflict with the old record dealer. Against all expectations, he almost chokes on the news.

"Oh boy! Are you sick or something?

- Don't worry, Selim. I accept the omen. Madness is my last resort. I'll take care of your personal problems, you see. I have a friend in Paris. I'll go and ask her for hospitality... Here comes the train... I'll be back soon.

- How can you laugh! Be reasonable. Be careful anyway... Give me a call if there's any news..."

Despite the delay caused by a false bomb threat at the Nice-Ville station, the train rushes on, then rushes into the tunnel that pierces the volcanic massif of Estérel, and its red porphyry cliffs. From there, my phone starts to crackle, it's Selim who says: "You, you're going to get smoked!"

***

December 15th, it's 9pm and here I am in the Latin Quarter of Paris with my best friend, Victoria, a nice lady from Paris, Vietnamese by origin.

As a matter of fact, she and I met at an ungrateful age, in 2003. That summer, my parents had sent me to the United Kingdom for a language course. Not to London, as I had hoped, but to Truro, a small town with Georgian architecture located in the heart of Cornwall, where Richard Lemon Lander of the band Queen grew up. So that's where I met Victoria, more precisely on the benches of the Truro School, where the actor John Rhys-Davies studied in his time, and whose motto is *"Esse Quam Videri"* ("Being rather than appearing"). What I discovered there, in such an intense way, remains forever intact, and will never leave my heart.

In the fifth disc, rue Mouffetard. This is the right place. How will this old crook react when he is informed of the object of my coming? Assailed by fatal presentiments, I stop on the threshold of the store. A silent horror breaks my courageous impulse. All reasonable people would say that what I am doing here is suicide! Between us, I fear to be scalped and to see my golden beard coming soon to add to the collection of hairpieces of André Bellaïche. Seeing me immobile, Victoria takes my arm : " Bah, go ahead, brother! What are you waiting for? It's freezing cold here!"

Victoria is the typical Parisian who, to escape the lynching of the "sans-dents" - I am one of them - participates in the regression of language by constantly using, to the point of plethora, inappropriate superlatives, but especially suburban barbarisms. I regain my courage, cross the threshold of Au cinquième disque, and walk up to a hairless giant with a bow tie, standing behind a cash register.

"Could you do me the grace of introducing me to Mr. Bellaïche?

- Who is asking?" asks the giant, in a surprisingly soft voice.

- It's only me, Oli, a sharp tintinophile, and a plumitif to boot, I say, with a salute.

- Is it indiscreet to ask you why you want to see him so badly?

- I have an important matter to discuss with him.

- Andre hasn't arrived yet, but he'll be here soon. It's only a matter of a dozen minutes or so..."

Now, Victoria and I are scouring the area, pretending to enjoy strolling around the fifteen or so bins of old vinyl records at knock-down prices, which form a makeshift barricade piled up in front of the entrance. The store is deserted. Not a single customer comes in. While waiting for him, I try to contemplate the 45 rpm displays, folding them down like dominoes with a heavy hand, and scattering a peppery dust that irritates my nostrils.

No record managed to capture my attention, with the notable exception of the soundtrack of the film *Sacco and Vanzetti*, signed by Ennio Morricone. This film tells the true story of two anarchist workers, of Italian origin, sentenced in the United States in 1927 to the electric chair for a crime they did not commit.

"Look out! Here he comes" says Victoria. On the road, it is André Bellaïche, helmeted, astride a scooter, holding between his legs a cornucopia full of copies of his book, piled up to the edge. The glow of the streetlights illuminates his face like the edge of a sword. He has grey eyebrows and a bushy salt-and-pepper moustache, lit by two brown eyes. I can hardly believe it. The terrible André Bellaïche, patron saint of hooligans! I am stunned. It is finally the voice of the giant who will come to sound the tocsin to remove me from my contemplative reveries. All piteous, and dripping, I advance towards him.

"Mr. Bellaïche, is it?", I said, after a moment of reflection, while drawing my right hand. Yes, that's me," he said in a slightly high-pitched voice, sticking his tongue out too far. And you, who are you? Oh! Oh! I think I saw a romin! Unbelievable but true, this dreadful rogue has a hair on his tongue. What a voice! Real wet rockets come out of his teeth. He speaks with a whistling accent, which makes him suddenly, as it is, very likeable.

My name is Oli," I said, "I am delighted to meet you. You see, I've been waiting for this moment for a long time. I'd like to buy this book, your autobiography... I've looked everywhere, but I can't find it.

- It is no longer published.

- Mr. Bellaïche, I have some extremely important things to tell you. May I speak to you here calmly?"

The introductions made, I solemnly bow, a little tased, and offer him a rough and hesitant hand. André Bellaïche, seeing it coming, first scrutinizes it with a round eye, behind his fine golden-mounted lorgnettes, as if trying to decipher the main lines.

"Ah! resumes the old Franco-Tunisian record dealer. It wants to talk business, eh? " Immediately, he bites the inside of his cheek, giving his face the effect of a dented relief, the eyebrows in circumflex accent. He finally decided to crush my phalanges. Who would have believed it! And then, releasing my hand to better smooth his moustache bristled by the cold at the point of the thumb and the index: "I am yours in a moment..."

And while André Bellaïche seizes the bridle of his steed to disappear at the bend of the street, in a thick cloud of smoke studded with spinning droplets, I regain the interior of the bazaar. "And then? Result?" questions me Victoria. Come on, come on! Be patient! Let us hope however that it returns, as promised. Need I remind you that the insane

Postiche is far from being a novice in the field of escape? On November 23, 1986, André Bellaïche managed to escape from the Roman prison of Rebibbia, Italy, aboard a Red Cross helicopter, just as Simon the Magician might have done, who, according to the Acts of Peter (32), seduced the crowd by flying to the heavens in Rome during the first century AD. Is it really a coincidence that the character who was supposed to represent André Bellaïche in the film *The Last Gang* was renamed Simon?

In front of me, the record player suddenly starts to play the celestial harmony *Come back baby* of Ray Charles. Enter André Bellaïche. A simple glance is enough to inform me about the man. He is not an ordinary man. Not very tall, full, square shoulders, large palms, patent black leather jacket, silver hair covered with gomina, elegantly thrown back, white shirt slightly indented, thick gold chain swinging on a bushy chest... He wears all the emblems of the Underworld according to a filmic reading grid. One would believe oneself in one of these scenes of which only Scorsese has the secret, and in which would appear the teigneous Joe Pesci.

André Bellaïche. - Here I am ready to hear you. What do you want from me?

Me, *the swollen chest* - If I am here today, it is to talk to you about Michel Fourniret. I happen to be friends with his son Selim.

André Bellaïche, *repressing a retching* - What! He is not dead yet, that one?

Me, *laughing yellow* - Oh, come on, sir. Selim is innocent. He has absolutely nothing to do with the crimes perpetrated by his parents.

André Bellaïche, *shouting with an irritated air* - Let him die! It's his son, after all. They are the same!

Me. - You misunderstand her, sir. You're completely wrong. Look, I know things about him and his father that might interest you. Will you allow me to discuss them with you?

At these words, the old record shop threw a shout, took his momentum, and ran straight into a wall. André le Mage has disappeared under curtains of vermeil crosses veiling a hidden door, made in a wall of cut stones. A plaintive rumor rises from the room. What threatening noises! The evocation of the only name of Fourniret was enough to excite all his fury. The giant, who had heard part of this dialogue, beckoned me not to move. I stop, struck with surprise. The last time a guy asked me to "wait", it was to better use his weapons against me, just after I had shattered his eyebrow. How could it be otherwise with a man of honor too smart to get caught? My interlocutor had been sentenced in the past to seven years in prison for receiving stolen goods! Even, during the umpteenth robbery that took place on rue du Docteur-Blanche in Paris on January 14, 1986, the Postiches had not hesitated to use gunpowder, leaving a CRS on the floor...

I am about to flee in a hurry when, suddenly, in the loudspeakers, a sweet voice coos. This voice is that of Ray Charles, intoning a melodious phrase, offering me the illusion that he is speaking directly to me: *"Oh! Come back, baby! Oh! mama please don't go, yeah!"* Suddenly, the bellowing subsides. André Bellaïche reappears, full of rage.

André Bellaïche, *handing me a bluish plastic bag* - Here is your book!

Me. - Are you sure you don't want to talk about Fourniret?

André Bellaïche. - What exactly do you want me to say?

Me. - Well, you know his story well, they say...

André Bellaïche, *pretending not to understand the allusion to his stolen treasure* - I asked you a question. What do you want me to tell you?

Me, *stubborn* - To begin with, I would like to know what you think of Fourniret...

André Bellaïche, *heaving a few plaintive sighs* - I don't think so! Apart from that, what else do you want me to say?

Me. - Good question! I'm confused, really.

André Bellaïche, *without ever saying Fourniret's name* - Pfff! You yourself don't know what you want to ask me! How would I know anything about him? I've never seen him in my life. I was in the carriage when he was there too. Again, what do you want to ask me?

Me, *trembling with emotion* - Very well! I'll tell you what I want to know. I'd like to know why Fourniret is never mentioned, either in your autobiography or in the screenplay of its film adaptation, *The Last Gang* with Vincent Elbaz.

André Bellaïche. - Why should I have mentioned his name?

I am. - For the simple and good reason that we know that he is the one who got the loot from the Postiches gang...

André Bellaïche, *with a deep indignation* - But, what do you know about it, you?

Me. - It's an open secret.

André Bellaïche, *pensive* - Okay! And according to you, how much did he take in that coffin? What? How much did he take?

The old record dealer has just distilled a precious detail about the burial of the booty, once buried at the bottom of the cemetery of Fontenay-en-Parisis, in the Val-d'Oise.

The Postiches would have elected a real coffin to house all their gold.

Me. - I will repeat what I have heard. According to the myth, the war treasure of the Postiches was composed of 34 ingots, 6,000 gold coins, and 80 kilos of jewels.

André Bellaïche, *laughing, not without a certain irony -* Hey what! Is that the treasure of the Postiches gang, in your opinion? Well, that gang must have been very sad! I don't want to talk about it. Frankly, I don't like it! I'm not talking about a scoundrel, a child killer, after all!

Me. - As you wish, sir. In any case, you should know that Michel Fourniret talks like a book. He repeats all sorts of things to his son in the letters he writes to him. So, perhaps we could...

André Bellaïche, *interrupting me -* But he does what he wants! I don't care about all that! No, no, no! I don't even want to know.

I am. - In any case, he does not have long to live. Nature will take care of the rest.

André Bellaïche. - Why? He has cancer, right?

Me. - Not yet, but prison has taken its toll. However, I dare to hope that time will do its work. That's what his son Selim wants too: for him to die. I guarantee it.

André Bellaïche, *signing the title page of the book I'm about to buy -* No but, frankly, do you realize who you want me to talk about? The worst kind of human being! It's like asking me about Hitler. I am a Jew! I'm Jewish!

Me, *lowering my eyes with shame -* Forgive my insolence. I just found it strange that at the end of the movie, well, you...

André Bellaïche. - Not at all! Fourniret has nothing to do with it!

Me, *calm and thoughtful* - Forgive me if I'm wrong, but during the final scene, we see you - well, I mean Simon - get out of prison, and conclude thus: "With my buddies, when we got out of prison, we wanted to recover the money we had stashed away, but it was all gone, like in my nightmare. And even though nobody suspected anyone, we never saw each other again." But finally? Why didn't you just say that it was Michel Fourniret who had double-crossed you?

André Bellaïche. - But since I tell you that Fourniret has nothing to do with it! Here! Why don't you go and question the Breton instead, eh?

Me. - Hellegouarch? He is Selim's godfather, you know. I read that he got his information from the Italian bank robber Gian Luigi Esposito, with whom you escaped from Rebibbia prison in 1986. Fatally, he had collected, it is said, the confidences of a member of the Postiches gang. Subsequently incarcerated at Fleury-Mérogis, Esposito would have given the whole story to Hellegouarch. Finally, Esposito was extradited to Italy. To recover the gold, the Breton, who knew where the Postiches had hidden their loot, called on another prison acquaintance: Michel Fourniret. All in all, it is the Breton who is responsible for this mess. Isn't it true?

André Bellaïche, *rough and ready* - It's not his fault. It's his gang, Fourniret, him, and all the rest! Besides, the poor guy's wife has disappeared...

At this moment, he seizes me by the collar, and slips slyly into my ear, in a tone of confidence, as if he had planned to thrust a Toledo rapier down my throat:

"Be careful who you go to when you go to ask these types of questions. A real thug will shoot you for less. You might get chilled stupidly. So to speak."

As a dedication, André Bellaïche writes in neat little handwriting, "Oli, I hope you will come out of *My Life without a hairpiece* without breaking and entering."

11.

VALENTINE'S DAY MASSACRE

"The more you step on the heads of the weak,
the more likely we are to lick the boots of the strong."
Tonino Benacquista

Saturday February 14, 2015 in Cannes

A week later, I meet Selim at the Wobben. He is very cheerful, sitting in front of a big bowl of Ardennes beer with a nice white foam. Without saying a word, I observe him with a curious eye. While I thought I could devote myself to the true and sincere story of my Parisian adventures, I find myself unable to place one. Selim confides to have given himself up to marauding, last night, during his hours of service at the supermarket. Tormented by a monster hunger, he would have left the checkpoint to rush into the detours of a maze of dark shelves, lit by his only flashlight.

"Hey what! Did you commit a petty theft? But why did you confess? You are guilty of stealing products for sale, aren't you?

- A little, yeah! A huge pot of crème caramel!" nods Selim, piling fried goujons and seasoned pork slices on his plate. I fulfilled everyone's dream: feasting in Ali Baba's cave, out of opening hours. Considering my salary, it's not stealing."

Selim would have thrown away his strangles, he who had never made such a mistake! I smile, stupidly. Of course, this is a peccadillo. The sullen boy of the beginning, closed like an oyster, is now opposed to the image of a budding adventurer, having taken a taste for risk.

Very well!" I exclaimed in my turn. I learned a lot of things in Paris... Since I listened to you speak very patiently, I announce you that...

- More of this, please, cut me off Selim, please!

- As you wish.

- After years of abstinence, I finally found love.

- Whoa, buddy!" I said, almost choking. What do you say? But finally, explain yourself!

- Yes, I have found love," he repeats with a sigh of relief.

- Admirable! And may I know who is the chosen one of your heart?

- It doesn't matter what his name is," the ogre's son replies curtly, eager to preserve this part of his intimacy with wonderful caution.

- Did you reveal your true identity to him?

- I give him all my confidence, therefore yes. Between her and me, I believe that it is gone to last, he prophesies, by wiping his face.

May you tell the truth, Selim! I exclaimed. For the record, I remind you of the instructions: of course, you are free to refuse, but as far as possible, don't talk about anything to do with your father, without first thinking about it. If you don't want the matter to be publicized, don't talk about it. This is my opinion."

Besides, rather than playing the ill-fated peddler, I chose to keep quiet about André Bellaïche's sinister predictions, the better to toast with enthusiasm to the happy news. Frankly, I could not see myself announcing to him that a famous gangster wanted to see him "die".

"Whoa! Helmsman! Three rounds of rum!"

In the following days, I conducted my little investigation on the beautiful girl. Her name is Hasna[14] . She is a pretty woman of North African origin with an attractive face, strawberry blond locks, and a lumbar arch in square. On social networks, she gives herself great airs of ass-benit, by publishing only Koranic verses, even photographs of her proudly wearing the hijab. No trace of Selim in her publications. However, the modest Hasna, who, by the way, seems to have fallen from the sky, does not hesitate to publicly display her disdain and her aversion towards the Jewish people and the French police. She even goes so far as to relay a conspiracy theory aimed at implying that the State of Israel would hide behind the terrorist attacks that recently bloodied the editorial offices of *Charlie Hebdo*, and the Hyper Cacher store at the Porte de Vincennes, on January 7 and 9, 2015, in Paris. This Hasna really doesn't inspire my confidence... To be honest, I think about the possibility that she could play a double game in order to extract some confidences on the pillow, and to get the treasure, probably for the account of small strikes.

To tell him about it, I met Selim at the Wooden. He was busy pecking at a hollow plate. The first reaction of

---

14. Its name has been changed.

the little prince of Sautou was to tease me about my squea-king grolles with every step I took under the effect of the water. "What is this chinese stuff?", he said, gratifying me with some unfriendly words. Ah! ah! Fortunately, I knew what to say to calm his ardor in a lasting way. "Tell me a little more about your girlfriend. I don't know anything about her," I said, "absolutely everything, except that she is frankly anti-Semitic. Come on, Selim, tell me everything. Ah, if you had seen her face! The backlash was terrible. He fell off his pedestal, his face prostrate. Selim handed me an open envelope made of kraft paper, from which I took out several sheets of paper, among which a white cardboard cleverly folded and cut. There was an inscription in pencil half erased by the stay in its packaging: "Hidden sentence n°1507: to want late is not to want".

Michel Fourniret, *to Selim* - The prison lieutenant informed me, during an interview, of your visit project. On this subject, if I am not opposed to it? I will use, by way of answer, the formula dear to my late father, Jules Louis Gaston Fourniret, born on May 8, 1899 in Moiry, in the Ardennes: "The fair is not on the bridge! Come to see me? You are free to be part of a group of spectators who squander their few pennies to come and feast their eyes. "Fuck! The beast in a cage?" You are free to offer yourself the double pleasure of the journey and the spectacle of the landscape. Add to this the sentence of the venerable Pierre-Paul Deschamps[15] of the lodge Les Frères unis inséparables du G.O.D.F.: "Everything is important. Nothing is important. We have time!"

---

15. Its name has been changed.

On the other hand, I am concerned about the consequences - in terms of physical effort - of moving from the Alpes-Maritimes to Alsace and back. Bus, train, walk... Where to stay? To eat ? And that's without mentioning the risk, for your neighbors in Vallauris, of being stunned by your "exhausted" appearance.

***

What exactly are these ideograms? I'm holding in my hand one of those damned out-of-print books of chivalry teaching us that the three dots are used in Masonic correspondence, and that G.O.D.F. means "Grand Orient de France". This letter is supposed to indicate Michel Fourniret's alleged membership in the Grand Orient de France? It is the oldest Masonic obedience, the most important in continental Europe...

"Do you happen to know why your father is referring to this association here?

- Yeah. It's a subject he's been passionate about for years. He used to brag about being a part of it. He would often allude to it at dinner time."

Suddenly, the image of Michel Fourniret, entangled in a blood-stained apron and holding a flaming sword in his white-gloved hand, floats in the air before me.

"And Pierre-Paul Deschamps, does that speak to you?

- How should I know?" roared Selim. I have nothing to do with those lunatics.

Pierre-Paul Deschamps? I can't see the point of this name. Deschamps? It's a French name, of course, but so what? In the meantime, I now know to whom is attributed this syllogism that Michel Fourniret took as his motto:

"Everything is important. Nothing is important. We have time!" How do I know if Deschamps really exists, or if this is just a polyptote to signify clues to us in the form of a cryptogram, like "polished stones in the fields"? Besides a check for 250 euros, a small greeting card caught my attention. It shows two red-headed waterfowl with webbed feet, all spotted with brown, crossed out with the following words: "With its 36 small centimeters long and 350 grams, the teal is the smallest duck in Europe. Why is Michel Fourniret trying to draw our attention to this ominous bird? Perhaps he finally understood that my dearest wish was to pluck Uncle Scrooge, before wringing his neck? At first glance, one might think that this note is not very useful. However, with hindsight, it seems almost obvious to me that the galley slave is trying to direct his son to a specific point on the map. Still, it must be a clue to the location of the loot...

Would it be possible to find palmipeds in the commune of Clairefontaine-en-Yvelines? I then scanned the map of the world, which was posted just above my desk, and I found several small pools of water in the peaty meadows, between the rue de Paincourt and the Impasse des Maisons-Blanches, where the Pavillon and Moulin ponds are located. This is without counting the numerous gullies that run in a star shape, all around the path known as the Bonnes Femmes, which is crossed perpendicularly by the path of the Orme. Is Michel Fourniret trying to draw our attention to the edge of the stagnant waters, where gold and perhaps a dead body would be plunged?

I proposed to Selim to write the following letter to his dear and tender father:

Selim, *to Michel Fourniret* - Stop taking me for a kid! You see, I'm not fifteen anymore. I've grown up since the last time. Indeed, I will soon visit you in Ensisheim. Beyond that, tell me a little about yourself, about your daily life in prison... Are you treated well? Did the other inmates never give you any trouble for what you did to those unfortunate children? Do you have a cellmate? Are you in contact with other prisoners? Michel, time is money. Fountain, I would gladly drink your water. Happy Valentine's Day under the soapy showers of the Ensisheim prison.

***

We attached to our new dispatch a receipt on which we circled in red pen the numbers seven and eight which, when put together, form the postal code of the "village of the Blues". Perhaps it would be prudent, as a matter of conscience, not to go alone to my next appointment. The senses fogged, I got up softly, very satisfied with the turn that my affair had taken, then I dragged Selim with me by the arm, trotting towards the exit door opening on the shiny pavement, where the first lights were already refracting after the storm.

12.

SPECIAL MACHINES

"Time spent with a cat is never lost."
Colette

May 23, 2014, in Ensisheim

On an ordinary spring morning, the sandy floor of my living room is littered with a profusion of blackened paperwork. Some of them are even hanging like a flag from a clothesline stretched on the terrace, sometimes slapped by the wind. As for the French window with small panes, this one is obstructed, in the same way, by an Ardennes tapestry with the Fourniret logo, leaving only a bucolic landscape in fragments to see outside. Seen from the floor where I am lying, one would almost think that the first snow has fallen... I have been trying for the last eight days to catch the meaning of his pleas, but there is nothing to be gained. When will Fourniret finish his useless harangues? Any effort to put together a cluster of clues leading to the treasure seems futile to me. In this joyous mess, in addition to a few objects - press clippings, "Femen" stamps - I came across a strange document bound with two strong staples, flanked by a symbol representing four arrows pointing to the center of a square, and bearing the title:

Central House Ensisheim
Synthesis co. - Sentence Execution Pathway (S.E.P.)
- May 26, 2014

Last name, first name : Fourniret Michel. Born on April 4, 1942. Arrival at the plant: June 2011. Sentence of life imprisonment. Life sentence (incompressible sentence). Already convicted reoffends.

From the first few pages, I understand that it is the classified report of prisoner n° 5451, directly from the prison administration. In it, there is everything we have always wanted to know about this madman, since he lives behind bars. It details his conditions of incarceration in Ensisheim, the activities he performs, and even contains - surprisingly - the results of a thorough psychological examination carried out by the deputy director of the prison. By what miraculous chance did this paper escape from prison and land in my home?

I even note the presence of handwritten annotations from the "ogre of the Ardennes": "Here, son," he writes with the tip of a badly sharpened gray pencil, "is enough to answer the few questions you raised in your last letter. A masterpiece of laconism.

That's it! I got it! This document must have been stuck at the bottom of the paper folder he had sent me, and that I had forgotten to empty. Here is the complete content of Michel Fourniret's prison file:

In detention. - Correct, discreet, solitary, he does not associate with anyone. He goes out on H3/H4 courses. He does not pose a discipline problem. He writes a lot. His cell is filled with papers. He writes on everything, even milk cartons... He stacks, aligns, classifies and labels in a strange way handwritten documents, but also newspapers, magazines, and all sorts of objects. There is no decoration in his cell, no hi-fi system, no computer. The only material in his possession: a television set.

Telephone: none // Parlour: none // Mail: no mail, but has been sending money to his son regularly for the past two months // Schooling: no contact // Professionally: unoccupied since his assignment to the plant - receives a pension of 600 euros // Accounting and voluntary payment civil party: YES, 336 euros per month since October 2013.

Summary of compensation. - 125 euros per month in March 2012 and suspension in April 2012. Payments in January, August and September 2011, about 2,000 euros compensated in 2011 - suspension of voluntary payments in October 2011.

Amount of damages: 1 039 740 euros

Amount compensated: 49,638 euros.

Passbook: 3,518 euros.

Mandate(s): retirement pension (600 euros per month)

Service pénitentiaire d'insertion et de probation (spip). He is 72 years old and retired. His contacts with his family are extremely limited. The contacts with his brother are limited to the settlement of administrative procedures. His family members have changed their names, suffering from his reputation. Although the wish of his family (son, ex-wife Nicole) is to keep his distance from him, Michel Fourniret nevertheless tries to get in touch with them [...] He sends money orders to his son, tries to send money orders to his ex-wife, and to his brother, these money orders come back.

He receives a pension. He spends most of his time (day and night) reading and writing. He occasionally goes out for a walk. He had a seizure of the guarantee fund in August 2013 (16,768.03 euros), following which he put back a voluntary payment of 336 euros from October 2013.

He admits to murder, but not to rape. He does not want a visitor in prison. He does not benefit from psychological or psychiatric follow-up. He does not request the SPIP, but he goes to every interview. He does not have any relationship with his fellow inmates.

Psychologically. - Michel Fourniret applies himself to lose foot with reality, by choice.

Assistant Director. *On detention and its behavior* - You are correct. We have a comment to make to you regarding the letters that are sent to us. When you send letters to the penitentiary staff, we would like you to be more concise in your writings because often, you clutter up your missives with considerations that are totally useless and futile, for example your digression in the form that you returned to us to inform us of your presence at the PEP commission.

Michel Fourniret. - I was in the Santé prison in Paris before I came here. It's not my intention to leave here. I don't write, it's my pencil that blackens the paper. My days are not long enough. As far as my letters are concerned, I don't care to have functional writings. I will be clear from now on. I would like to point out that I walk to maintain my physical fitness.

Michel Fourniret. *On the civil parties* - I have no merit in this. I took the lead.

Michel Fourniret. *On his psychological follow-up* - No psychological or psychiatric follow-up. I don't feel the need. It is not my intention.

Assistant Director. - The relationship with his peers is limited. He lives in seclusion, next to others. He does not interact with his fellow inmates. He voluntarily isolates himself.

Michel Fourniret. - Social cohabitation is not my concern. I only meet others if they need help. Meeting my victims has put me in impossible situations, or in front of a chessboard. You know, even though I am a person who withdraws, I don't try to spare myself from suffering, otherwise I wouldn't suffer from chronic insomnia.

***

"Michel Fourniret applies himself to losing his footing with reality, by choice [...] When you send letters to prison staff, we would like you to be more concise in your writings because often you clutter your missives with considerations that are totally useless and futile to us." Clearly, I am not alone in thinking that the prisoner grants himself the title of writer. Before resuming my hard work, I make sure that Colonel Mizu has a sufficiently ample supply of kibble.

***

Michel Fourniret gave us an important tip. I couldn't help but investigate the name Pierre-Paul Deschamps. Who the hell is this P.P.D.? The answer is most uncertain... Besides, here is the only information I could gather. It turns out that the lodge Michel Fourniret refers to in his letter - Les Frères unis inséparables - was founded in Versailles on August 1st, 1775. I learned from my readings and conversations that the ogre lived in this same department from 1966 to 1984, more precisely in Clairefontaine-en-Yvelines, but also in Rambouillet.

Better still, throughout its history, according to some sources, the lodge has counted among its members illustrious luminaries, such as the kings Louis XVI, Louis XVIII, Charles X, or the composers Rodolphe Kreutzer and Giacomo Meyerbeer. All this to finally see the ogre appear on the stoop and ask for an audience with the roofer brother? What a revolution! But in the end, is it so surprising when you know that the pedophile who thought he was a king also lived the life of a castle in Donchery, starting in 1988?

At the end of 1987, despite his sentence of seven years in prison, two of which were suspended, and three years of probation for raping minors under the age of 15, Michel Fourniret was released from Fleury-Mérogis, and then left to start a new life with Monique Olivier in the Yonne region, in Saint-Cyr-les-Colons. On the other hand, according to the newspaper Le *Monde* in its edition of January 9, 2006, it is precisely at this period that would have begun his career as a murderer. He does not say everything," said Didier Seban, lawyer for the Desramault family, just before the opening of the trial on March 27, 2008. During previous hearings, Michel Fourniret stated that he had killed two to three victims per year since his release from prison in 1987.

If we assume that Michel Fourniret told the truth, before recanting, and that he was arrested in June 2003, there should be about 16 victims, which is surprising, since the justice system's counter has stopped at seven, notwithstanding about 30 unknown DNAs found on some 4,000 hairs found in the back of his van.

In view of this chronology, a question arises: Pierre-Paul Deschamps, could it be that you knew about the machinations of the strangler at the time? I want to know, but I can't even say if this P.P.D. is still alive. There is certainly a good reason why he repeats so many times to Selim this proverbial phrase, which he attributes to P.P.D.: "Everything is important. Nothing is important. We have time!"

I think it is appropriate to launch into some in-depth research on this individual, taking care, however, not to arouse particular suspicions unnecessarily. The above-mentioned individual would be at the head of a medical biology analysis laboratory known as Labo-Test, near Vanves, a city located in the southwest of Paris.

In another letter, Michel Fourniret directly refers to Pierre-Paul Deschamps as his "client in the study and realization of special machines". Michel Fourniret does indeed present his mentor as his "client", which seems to suggest that he would have carried out an order in return for payment of a fee. What does he call "machine"? What does he call "special"?

Nothing, absolutely nothing specifies here what kind of service the "ogre of the Ardennes" could bill to this mysterious Deschamps... What is certain, on the other hand, is that this guy has never been questioned on this subject by the investigators. However, we know that the changeover took place in the Yvelines. Everything leads us to believe that he might have been in contact with Michel Fourniret at the very moment when the latter was starting to implement his "drawer" plan. Maybe he knew, *de facto*, that something was going on, or maybe there are only coincidences here... We are talking about murdered children, and not vulgar "machines" without soul.

One day, I took advantage of a simple conversation over an enchanting beer at L'Almira Wobben to bring the subject to the table, without going into too much detail.

"Psst! Selim, do you remember, by any chance, if Michael had any... friends?

- And how! Yes, many, but I wouldn't be able to name any. I was so young. I wasn't interested in that kind of thing...

- When you were in Belgium," I said, "was it usual to receive visits from these people?

- Yes, they were local guys, for the most part. From time to time, we also went to visit some people on the other side of the border. Hey there! One name comes to mind! I think it was one of his first bosses... A guy named George, I think, or something like that. I'm not sure of the name, of course... I know it sounds strange, but I don't know my parents.

In the early 1960s, Georges - now deceased - distinguished himself as the first employer of the "ogre of the Ardennes". As the owner of a metalworking factory, he opened his arms to him by hiring him as a milling worker. On Tuesday, May 6, 2008, before the Ardennes Assize Court, Michel Fourniret had to face Dominique, Georges' daughter. All this was an opportunity for her to recall the memory of her late father in the face of the serial killer, for whom he had literally taken a liking: "Dad taught you great values: love of one's neighbor, respect of people. Make sure you respect him", she had reminded him, before summoning him to confess: "Tell the truth!" In his glass cage, hands clutching the edge of the box, Michel Fourniret, with a discouraged look on his face, almost fell out of his chair, and addressed these few words to her: "I cannot. Otherwise I would do it[16].

Besides, Pierre-Paul Deschamps remains untraceable. I have not found the slightest proof of his existence, except for the presence of this name in a few letters from the serial killer. I tried to contact all the Deschamps listed in the Vanves directory, but nothing came of it. One potential witness to Fourniret's mutation, apart from Monique Olivier - and now he is nowhere to be found, lost in the wild!

In the daily newspaper *L'Yonne républicaine of* July 7, 2004, journalist Hubert Besson asked: "What networks are involved in the Fourniret case? [...] But how could he have acted without other accomplices, without networks, when the number of misdeeds he committed would have been far greater than those of an Emile Louis or a Marc Dutroux? Why could he have acted as a quiet father, almost as a loner, when the killers we have reported on needed to rely on networks?"

The same is true of the controversial association Wanted Pedo, from which I received this message: "If you do some research on Michel Fourniret, you will see that he has been protected for a long time. In spite of everything, they tried to sell him to us as a professional chess player who managed to slip through the cracks for a long time." According to the official version, it is however attested that between 1987 and 2001, the "Ogre of the Ardennes" operated alone, in company with Monique Olivier.

While reading, I discovered a detail of great importance, but which has since been forgotten. Among the most

---

16. See the article by Yves Bordenave, "Michel Fourniret collapses, in tears, in front of the daughter of his first boss", in *Le Monde* of May 7, 2008.

12. Special machines

important leads favored by the investigators following the disappearance of twelve-year-old Elisabeth Brichet near Namur on December 20, 1989, there is that of a man named Jean-Marc Houdemont. This Belgian filmmaker, who had an attraction for young girls and pornography, was killed in a car accident on February 25, 1997, when he was on his way to make revelations to the investigating judge in Namur, in the context of the Brichet case, of which it will later be known that she was brutally murdered by Selim's father. Elisabeth's body was finally found in 2004, at the Sautou castle. Yes, she was raped, then strangled. Jean-Marc Houdemont? Died halfway along the path to redemption?

To this I will add nothing. My role should not be confused with that of a policeman, or a judge, all driven by emotion. Because, finally, I share the old French taste for Justice, the real one. There is a dramatic interest there. Besides, I think I have sown enough clues. Depending on the goodwill of the competent authorities, the possibility will open up of a new avenue of investigation into Fourniret, and his "special machines", likely to probe the mystery of this case, which is still so far from being entirely solved.

Let the police do their job. For my part, I bet there's still something rotten in the kingdom of Sautou, as William Shakespeare might have said. Who knows how many corpses of abandoned children are still rotting in secret places?

13.
WHIPLASH

> "The real did not happen".
> Michel Onfray

October 11, 2015 in Nice

Five long months have passed. We have been able to awaken the old demons, but nothing has happened. The competent authorities had assured me that the Farida Hammiche case would be resolved before the end of 2015. However, the Court of Appeal of Yvelines is now passing the buck with the High Court of Charleville-Mézières, officially dispossessed of the case since 2007. Where on earth has the Fourniret case really gone? I think it got stuck in the dilapidated plumbing of the Ministry of Justice...

This doubt was confirmed by Gregory Vavasseur, Michel Fourniret's lawyer, for whom the situation is not about to change any time soon: "Oh, that! The case is dragging on. No trial date has been set, on the grounds that the case is still under investigation. However, I note a total inactivity of the investigators. The case is buried. No judge is in a hurry to deal with such a thick file. Yet there is no great mystery, since confessions about the disappearance of Farida Hammiche were made by Michel Fourniret in the wake of his arrest. Except that it was thirty years ago! This is a real shame for Justice. It all makes no sense.

I contact Selim again. An appointment is set for the next afternoon around 4 pm, at the Almira Wobben. When the clock strikes two, I receive an e-mail from him, containing a link to a five-minute report entirely devoted to domestic rabbits. Ah, here is another proof, no doubt, of his unbearable punster humor. When Selim mentions the rodent mammal, it's just a way of expressing his fear of being "stood up" by me.

The night passes, and the next day, at the appointed hour, I invest the place du Pin. Twenty-five minutes late, the tall, gangly-looking man arrived with his arms flailing on the curb.

- Hey! Giacometti! How are you ?

- Oli," Selim said firmly, "there is something you need to know, something no one else knows.

- Here, here! Let me guess. You had a fight with the lady?

- To tell the truth, Hasna and I are finished", he grumbles with spite, his face closed.

Without any transition, Selim starts to display a whole series of photos showing the fawn-like face of a young girl, out of breath, with all four irons in the air, and her ass over her head. The bun undone, a cascade of rust-colored hair crossed her forehead. "But what does it all mean, Selim? Another notable fact, the nymphet in question is clasped by two large arms covered with a light black down. My word!" I exclaimed afterwards, "isn't that

Hasna in the nude? Of course it is, it's her, "figure you that I discovered the pot in the roses, Selim resumes. She always cheated on me".

What's up! Hasna, a girl from nothing? So, wasn't I right?

"What she has always wanted most is to marry me with the sole purpose of obtaining French nationality and to bring into the country the man who happens to be her real fiancé, also Algerian. A grey marriage! Hasna has never lived in France. I lied to you. She came on to me on a dating site, that's how our relationship started. All in all, I have only seen her three times in my life... The border police had warned me, Selim confesses, in a monotone more dramatic than then. They contacted me by phone at the beginning of the year for a hearing about our marriage project, and Hasna's comings and goings in France. One day, they had informed me of a potential risk in this direction. What an idiot I am!

- Hey! Marriage, you say? My ass! No, come on, you can't be serious, Selim. Pacs, you mean, don't you? No ? Wait, are you telling me that you were going to marry an Algerian girl, gleaned from the Internet, that you've only seen three poor times in your life?"

Selim responds affirmatively with a nod of his head. "I wanted to start a family. I really believed in it, you see...". At the sight of the pornographic photos displayed without modesty, a waiter particularly in verve, appears at our table, throwing, mocking: "Oh, the bitch! Hm! Sorry...", he says, putting our glasses on the table. More serious disgrace, I understand that once again, the son of the "ogre of the Ardennes" has been used as bait. It is terrible. What lesson can be drawn from this new failure if not that, despite all his efforts, Selim is, after all, the victim of a family curse. After lunch, Selim gives me a bill, a little crumpled. Since he has not received any more answers from us, Mich-Mich has stopped sending money orders. Nothing, for at least three months. In his last letter dated July, the tone became harsher. On the bill, by way of introduction, the "ogre of the Ardennes" crossed out the word "son" from his manuscript, and replaced it with "sir" in red marker.

Michel Fourniret, *to Selim* - Son sir, communicating vessels effect. "Give and you shall receive". As a result: given your complacency to ramble, I have no choice but to: slow down, reduce, even cut the bridges! Message over. And this, you little prick, on the strength of the media crap! No more indulgence in gratuitous ravings. I'm sorry.

***

A curious package is attached to Fourniret's bill. A used toothbrush, vacuum-packed, and decorated at each end with a head blackened by grime. It is flanked by the acronym B.A.D.P.G.G. which, when spelled out, means: "Toothbrush for big mouths". Usually, such flowery language is hardly used from Fourniret. Here he waves his tentacles armed with prickles, unrolls them from the depths of his thebaid to try to inflict a good correction on his son. The latter, forgetting his sempiternal stoicism, straightens up, as if struck by lightning: "It is finished with the mandates-cash, repeats Selim, with a vile swearword. I've had enough of chewing on the ogre's teats! I don't need his pity to pay my bills. It's the carrot or the stick." Removing the protective cap from the ballpoint pen tip by pulling it down, Selim draws a stigma on the palm of his left hand, checking its functionality.

Selim, *to Michel Fourniret* - Dad, Michel, you complain to have been offended? You're making a fuss over a simple mammal! But, how dare you? But, who do you think you are? According to you, how do you get respect? I saw an interesting program about you. It was about rabbits. And this is what it said:

The rabbit is the favorite animal of children. So how do you take care of your rabbit? The answer: the small cage is suitable for rabbits. Always choose a cage with bars. A Plexiglas cage creates a greenhouse effect. The rabbit is a small animal that only breathes through its nostrils. A small animal with sensitive airways. The "hay of convenience" you mention represents seventy percent of the rabbit's diet.

I ask here a simple question, which is directly addressed to the cuistre of the Ardennes: are you stupid to eat hay? The arrest warrant was followed by the cash warrant, then by silence. Now, don't forget that the eternal mark of the plural is the "X", well before the "S".

***

On a personal note, the newly spurned and disillusioned lover wishes to let his father believe that his love life is going well, so much so that he would even consider sealing his union with a purely imaginary being.

Selim, *to Michel Fourniret* - Today, I have my own apartment, I have my job and, above all, I'm going to get married soon. But you'd know all that if you bothered to check up on me in your ubiquitous letters, full of useless remarks and flashes that fall flat. I'm not a child anymore, not a kid.

By Lucifer! Michou, tell me where did the other cherubs who crossed your path crash? Answer me, you infamous nerd, without adding a gloss! Where on earth do you find the courage, and the pride to keep on breathing?

***

Finally, I confide in Selim about my intention to push his father into a corner, to the point of turning his violence against him. He starts to stammer, then gets hold of himself and says: "If he dies, it will not make me hot or cold. Whether he lives or dies will not change anything that has happened. The dead won't come back. Who knows? Maybe the relatives of the victims will feel relieved, so be it.

Thus we load our Chekhov's rifle[17] with a first silver bullet, materialized here in the form of a new illustration: an earthworm skewered at the end of an attractive hook, a heavy trout endowed with a most voracious appetite. This small drawing is then superimposed in relief on the text in the form of a folded collar, the base of which is fixed by a ruddy sticker cut into two parts glued upside down, but which, if they are glued back together, distinctly articulates the following message: "Life is in the blood", which happens to be the slogan of the tenth World Blood

---

17. Chekhov's rifle is the dramaturgical device where an element introduced very early in the story does not see its interest become clear until much later. For example, a character may find a mysterious object that will ultimately become crucial to the plot; but at the time of its discovery, the object does not seem important.

Donor Day. May it all end soon!" sighs Selim. Ah, at least," I exclaimed, quoting Ovid, "let us not die without vengeance!"

Finding it too bitter for his taste, the prince of Sautou spits out a fillet of Negroni, which will be spread at the bottom of the act marked with this seal: "The bait having been used for a long time for the traps of the pedophile rabbit drawn from the hat of a magician, whose name is kept secret. Perhaps P.P.D. and his special machines".

14.
Casus Belli

> "War is the best opportunity
> to make crap.
> It gives permission."
> Erri De Luca

October 18, 2015 in Nice

The first harpoon fell on me last July, in the form of a strange phone call from the Brigade de répression de la délinquance contre la personne (B.R.D.P.). On the other end of the line, from Paris, a voice introducing herself as Brigadier Bérengère[18] , announced that I was the target of a complaint for facts of "dissemination of images infringing on privacy", following the publication of a file in April 2015. To my great surprise, the brigadier wanted to send me a questionnaire to be returned to her duly filled in electronically, and this, at the request of the deputy public

---

18. The name has been changed.

prosecutor at the Paris court of first instance. "I was astonished to hear that a police interrogation by e-mail was really possible.

Finding the procedure surreal, and suspecting a vengeful prank, I proposed to the presumed gendarme to postpone our discussion, to give me time to conduct my little investigation. It did not fail! At the Paris police headquarters, an agent confirmed my doubts, certifying that an electronic hearing had "no legal value", and describing the method as "strange and unheard of". I refocused my research on this policewoman. The said Berengaria is, in fact, an actress, and was even a technical consultant for the needs of the series *Julie Lescaut*. Monique Olivier would be happy to learn this, she who, according to Selim, is an unconditional admirer of the investigations of this famous police commissioner of TV fiction...

Before cutting off this discussion, I followed the advice of the old sages by brandishing, as a protective shield, the law of January 4, 2010 on the protection of the secrecy of sources, which stipulates "that the secrecy of sources may not be directly or indirectly infringed unless there is an overriding public interest imperative to do so, and if the measures envisaged are strictly necessary and proportionate to the legitimate aim pursued. This infringement may in no case consist of an obligation for the journalist to reveal his sources".

While I was busy clearing the site of the Fourniret case, a second harpoon hit me. I was summoned to the gendarmerie of Saint-André-de-la-Roche, three leagues from my home, in order to be heard in the framework of an investigation on my supposed actions. In spite of the grotesque character of the methods employed, the announcement of a complaint lodged against me was thus not at all a hoax.

Tired of my silence, the B.R.D.P. gave the hot potato to the local gendarmerie. For some comic opera actors who have not succeeded in leading a life of strass and glitter, wielding a truncheon is a great way to make ends meet...

Around 2 p.m., on a pale afternoon, I go to the Poulaga house, where I am received by the adjutant R. In his office, he seems to be busy dusting some knick-knacks on his desk, including an advertising sign with the Cochonou logo. A curious debate about the freedom of the press ensued. The gendarme mistreats me in words. He displays the eight-pointed deer antler grenade and bludgeons me with increasingly incisive and personal questions, such as "what is the origin of your name?", or "what does your prison flower represent?

At this interrogation, with his hands hanging over a dusty keyboard, Warrant Officer R. waits patiently for me to give him the *word to* transcribe each of my unfortunate words on his computer, which is humming loudly:

Let's see, sir, I don't see the connection," I said. Yes or no, are you going to tell me why you sent for me? That's what I'd like to know..."

Three minutes later, the gendarme hands me a sheet of paper and asks me to sign my statement. Well," he says, "I don't congratulate you. I don't congratulate you. It's full of spelling mistakes," I said grudgingly. Oh, yes, and quite a few!

I end up signing the aforementioned document, eager to get it over with as quickly as possible. As I put the pen away at the bottom of a pencil cup erected in the middle of pastis cakes, a deep sigh of deliverance escapes me at the idea of being able to get away. We both leap to our feet, then move into the next room. Before letting you leave," he hastily explains, grabbing a large camera and pointing it at me, "I have to enter you in the database of the Criminal Records Processing (CRP). This procedure astonishes me and leaves me stunned. "Now stand against the wall with your chin up," the pandora orders me, applying his eye to the eyepiece. Terror takes hold of my mind. What will they do with me? My mouth begins to tremble. "I protest! I protest! Tell me, do I have the right to object, and to leave right now?" I stammer, my eyes trembling. "Ah, yes, you can," replied the adjutant, pulling on his blue polyester polo shirt. On the other hand, comrade, I prefer that you know," he continues, revealing sharp little teeth, "people who refuse to be registered can be imprisoned for up to six months and fined 15,000 euros. Afterwards, it's up to you... It's up to you! "Well! too bad," I said, with a resigned nod, my mouth agape. "Watch out! The little bird is going to come out!"

It had to be like that, he shoots me at point-blank range, from every possible angle... From now on, these few well-made shots will allow a system based on facial recognition software to formally identify me, under the eye of the Barbarians, as soon as my seven orifices have been detected by the video surveillance cameras installed everywhere in the streets of the country. A city like Nice is equipped with 1,256 high definition cameras.

"Now, I also need to take your fingerprints, and palm prints", announces the sergeant R., piously invoking the National Automated Fingerprint File (F.N.A.E.G.), as well as the Automated Fingerprint File (F.A.E.D.). Amazing! He grabs my wrists, as if to check my pulse, which is beating rapidly, then drags them with all his weight into the depths of an inking box. So here I am, officially on file with the government. All this for a simple article published in a poor tabloid? Either I'm wrong, or a System man has just used this false pretext to hang me from a peg. No doubt a clear message intended to calm my cursed thirst for gold…

At the end of this torture session, my torturer, all dressed in blue, grabs me with both hands on my shoulders, leads me back to the door, laughing under his breath, and I tell him:

"Who has commissioned you to do this sad task?

- Go! Don't play innocent! he hisses, between his scattered snags. I have the impression that you didn't expect to be welcomed like this, right? But you know that better than I do. You journalists think you can do anything! You deserve that…

- Hey, what?" I protested against the affront that had just been made to my corporation. Allowed? Do I think I can do anything? A journalist like me? For the last time, goodbye.

Behind me, the swinging doors slam with a noise similar to a whip. It will be necessary to quickly gather my scattered thoughts, in order to understand the scene which has just been played.

But what's the big deal? It's not like I'm about to commit the heist of the century, is it? However, this interrogation followed by this undignified file produce in me the expected effect, namely a slavish fear. What a frustration! I see it as a direct incitement to transgress the ban, which is the heart of the problem, because who better than slaves to dream the sweet dream of freedom?

***

The case in question concerns the nephew by marriage of an illustrious enarque who reached the highest positions in the government. I had the opportunity to meet him a few years ago around a table set up on the pebbles of a private beach of the Promenade des Anglais, during the presidential pre-campaign of 2011.

In September 2015, I published in the press an investigation concerning him, and aiming to sow doubt on the sincerity of his declaration of assets, due to the omission of some real estate on the Cannes side. Of course, I will not reveal the identity of the protagonists of this sad story. It is not important to know the name of my detractor, as long as it is well distinguished. Only the facts matter. Also, I will call hereafter his nephew, "Malgache".

It turns out that by a providential coincidence, my beloved Fanny is friends with "Malgache", the kind of cold-blooded nobleman who willingly gives himself the air of an adventurer, convinced that the fact of having traveled to Third World countries at the taxpayer's expense would have added to his lousy I.Q. In short, they both know each other rather well, having once attended the private school of applied arts in Toulouse. As is customary, this gentleman of fortune comes every year to celebrate Christmas with his family, in Mougins, in a sumptuous residence, the very one targeted by my investigation... It is on this occasion that Fanny and him recently met for a drink, to evoke their memories, or at least, that is what she thought. "Malgache" was not there as a courtesy call. He had discovered our affair. The following words were told to me word for word by Fanny, during a conversation we had on my return from Monaco.

Well!" cried the nephew of one of the most unpopular politicians of his time. Who is this Oli Porri Santoro who is harassing my family? He took the liberty of ringing our doorbell three times, can you imagine? He has long been a great concern to us." At these words, I quickly realized that I might be the only one responsible for the misfortune that has befallen me. Ah, so it was me...

Terrified of getting into trouble because of me, Fanny snapped: "Why did you have to stick your nose in their business? Good for you. You embarrassed me. Now he thinks we're conspiring together. They really didn't like what you wrote about them, but not at all... They didn't see it coming, they are known for their discretion. They would like to know how you managed to get all this information, and where you got that picture from their private collection to illustrate your article."

What I wouldn't do to offend propriety? Besides, it intrigues me, especially since three months ago, my profile on the said social network suffered a targeted computer attack. My entire email was combed through. That's too much! For all these reasons, I bet that my inscription on the T.A.J. file is the price to pay for my "very big mistake", I should not have been too interested in the turpitudes of these "honest people" of the high society. It's true, this journalist, what a lack of education!

15.
IN THE LION'S MOUTH

"Always keep your friends close,
and your enemies, even closer."
Mario Puzo

November 11, 2015, in Nice

In Marseille, on July 28, 1976, Christian Ranucci, a twenty-two year old salesman from Nice, was the first person sentenced to death during the seven-year term of Valéry Giscard d'Estaing, and the last in France. Ten years before the day I was born, unable to inspire the slightest empathy, he was guillotined for the murder of an eight-year-old girl named Marie-Dolorès Rambla, in the Baumettes prison, the same one where Don Salvatore is currently detained. Ranucci, a Niçois? Good grief! I didn't know that, of course... It's strange!

The facts: on Monday, June 3, 1974, eight-year-old Marie-Dolorès Rambla was abducted from her apartment building in the Saint-Agnès housing estate in northeastern

Marseille. Her body, bruised with knife wounds, was found two days later, lying under brambles and broom. His face was unrecognizable. In a nearby mushroom farm, the investigators discovered an almost new red sweater. It is the first piece of evidence to be added to the file. In Nice, Christian Ranucci was arrested in his mother's apartment, based on the testimony of a couple of motorists after an ordinary traffic accident, and then transferred to Marseille. Never convicted, his criminal record was clean. The scratched forearms, and the muddy pants, he recognizes then the accident, but not the murder. After nineteen hours in police custody, it's the final straw. Under the blows of the police, Christian Ranucci collapses in full interrogation. He confesses to the crime, then recants, but it doesn't matter. The judicial machine is in motion, guided by the confession he has just signed. The trial opens on March 9, 1976, in Aix-en-Provence. It lasted only two days. The deliberation lasted only two hours. In *Le Figaro* of March 11, 1976, it was reported that Ranucci defended himself poorly, and that the sentence was passed "despite the doubts and unexplored leads. The President of the Republic Valéry Giscard d'Estaing, contrary to his convictions and promises, did not pardon Ranucci. "I am innocent!" proclaimed the condemned man as he walked to the guillotine. He died on July 28, 1976. Still according to this same article, which has reached us since the last century, "the death penalty is not a surprise, when one knows how much weight public opinion had on these debates. The jurors in Aix were sensitive to it. Moreover, one would have had to be blind and deaf not to see the inscriptions calling for death on the very walls of the courthouse and not to hear the crowd besieging our precinct, transformed into an entrenched camp, which was protected by large police forces...". To read it, this investigation reeks of haste, and Ranucci would have been handed over to a revanchist crowd that demanded his head, and this, with the sole purpose of dissipating tensions. Another notable fact is that it was the famous Judge Michel, known for having been at the forefront of the dismantling of the "French Connection," who was charged with closing the Christian Ranucci investigation file, which he knew to be fragile and full of huge gaps. In this regard, he is said to have confided to his deputy prosecutor friend, Etienne Ceccaldi: "It's a shitty case! Anxious to clarify what he considered to be grey areas, he was, according to some sources, prevented from doing so by his hierarchy, and ordered to close this file as soon as possible. Subsequently, he witnessed the execution of Ranucci on July 28, 1976, and was himself shot three times in 1981 with a 9 mm pistol.

Indeed, the investigation of little Dolores reveals many shortcomings. First, the witnesses of the kidnapping do not recognize Christian Ranucci. Secondly, the car of the kidnapper, a Simca 1100, is not his, and the famous red sweater discovered on the scene of the crime, which allowed the police dog to find the body of the victim, does not belong to him either. It is too big for him, and he never wears red. Even more disturbing, in another city of Marseille, a man wearing a red sweater and driving a Simca 1100 would have accosted children, the days before the abduction of Marie-Dolorès Rambla. According to many witnesses, this man was not Christian Ranucci.

In 1978, in a counter-investigation entitled *The Red Sweater*, the writer Gilles Perrault proclaimed Ranucci's innocence. For Gilles Perrault, there is no doubt: "We are

15. In the lion's mouth

condemned to doubt until the end. French justice will never dare to reopen this case, which has become a state truth. I hope that one day we will know the truth. I am firmly convinced that Ranucci was innocent.

Let's proceed in order. Forty years ago in Marseille, this man from Nice was guillotined for the murder of Marie-Dolorès Rambla. For thirty years, it will never be possible to put a name on the suspect with the Simca 1100 and the red sweater, or at least, until a certain Michel Fourniret appears on the scene, in January 2006. Strange... Is he the author of the girl's murder? It is only a hypothesis. It is not based on any scientific data, but it is taken very seriously in Belgium. However, in France, it is quite different, the hypothesis has not even been taken into consideration.

However, during a hearing, the "Ogre of the Ardennes" gave a major clue to the Belgian investigators. In 1974, the year of the murder of the little Rambla girl, when he claims to have passed through the region of the Etang de Berre, he was thirty-two years old. Like Ranucci at the time, he was the owner of a Peugeot 304. Another important detail: Michel Fourniret was already known, at that time, for molesting very young girls. His presence in the Marseille area, the same type of car, a similar psychological profile, these are all interesting elements, but very tenuous.

It is then that the illumination occurs in February 2006, with the irruption of a striking look-alike of Michel Fourniret, whom we will nickname "Esau", because there is in him something of a conspirator. Remember this name well: Esau. Pictures taken during the trial of Christian Ranucci in 1976, straight from the archives of the newspaper *La Provence*, show a man who could be Michel Fourniret. For obscure reasons, the newspaper categorically refuses to publish these photos of our lady Babushka[19], and even less to sell them. A newspaper which refuses to inform its readers, while earning money, it is not commonplace, you will agree. In any case, in April 2006, an anthropometric study concluded that it was not the serial killer. According to the prosecutor, "three points" make it possible to affirm that Fourniret is not the man of the photograph: the chin "with dimple" for Esau, not for Fourniret, the eyebrows of "falling type" for Esau, not for Fourniret, and the fact that it is established that the ogre did not carry glasses at the time of the trial Ranucci, contrary to Esau...

"Surprising," remarked ironically journalists from the RTL-TVi channel. The *Reporters* team's observation is edifying: "Today in France, reopening the Ranucci affair is a priority neither for the press nor for the justice system. No one has the intention of reopening the wounds."

Against all logic, these mysterious photos are kept out of reach of the public. In Charleville-Mézières, Francis Nachbar, the public prosecutor in charge of the Fourniret case, has seen them. According to him, Belgium sent a false S.O.S. "We were sent these photographs," he confirmed, still very sarcastic. We immediately made the very subjective comparisons between the photographs of Michel Fourniret at the same time, and that of the person who attended the Ranucci hearing. We were unanimous in saying that it was obvious that it was not at all the same individual. And to add with unbelievable arrogance: "If I am mistaken, and the

---

19. Lady Babushka is the nickname given to an unknown woman who was present at the assassination of John F. Kennedy and who may have filmed the events in Dealey Plaza in Dallas at the time the President of the United States was shot. Her nickname is directly related to the fact that she was wearing a scarf usually worn at the time by elderly Russian women. She was filming the murder scene. Lady Babushka and her film were never found.

15. In the lion's mouth

technical expertise will say so, well! I would immediately rush to an ophthalmologist because obviously, I would need to change my glasses. If I am not mistaken, as I have a strong feeling I will advise my colleagues who have seen disturbing similarities to also rush to the ophthalmologist, because you should not let your eyesight deteriorate too long. You have to take the problem as far upstream as possible."

What contempt for his Belgian counterparts! For Gilles Perrault, such a decision was predictable. Here is what he said in 2006, when questioned on RTL-Tvi: "It is obvious that you will not find a single policeman or magistrate in France who is overjoyed at the idea that Fourniret may be the real culprit, and that an innocent man was guillotined. It's an understandable corporatist reaction. I would say that French justice, which is in a very bad way at the moment with the Outreau affair, cannot afford the unheard-of scandal of a 22-year-old boy being beheaded when he was innocent. Valéry Giscard d'Estaing, the president of the Republic at the time who refused his pardon, who sent Ranucci to the scaffold, is still alive... You can imagine that granting a retrial to Christian Ranucci would be a political, legal and judicial earthquake.

According to the police, the case is closed. But obviously, this is not the opinion of this Belgian magistrate, who took care to appoint an *ad hoc* representative to find Michel Fourniret. What to do? What if the Belgian magistrate was telling the truth? Let's remember that the mysterious character with the red sweater and the Simca 1100 could never be identified.

Suddenly, I feel all the fires of hope revive in me. We can therefore expect, on this side, sensational discoveries which will be - one suspects - of a prodigious interest for justice.

16.
CRIME OF APOSTASY

> "Goodness gracious!" said Mr. Seguin;
> "But what are we doing to my goats?
> Another one that the wolf is going to eat me..."
> Alphonse Daudet, *Mr. Seguin's Goat*

November 14, 2015, in Nice

Selim Fourniret could have chosen another moment than the day after November 13 to announce his conversion to Islam. Such a thing cannot be invented. In these times troubled by obscurantism, the son of the serial killer Michel Fourniret, known for his alleged obsession with the Virgin Mary, attests that there is no divinity apart from Allah, and that Mohammed is his messenger, at a time when the opinion is moved by the massive departure of young Europeans, candidates for jihad, to the armed camps of Syria.

All this is quite mysterious coming from the prince of Sautou who, usually, abounds in phlegm. One wonders if he has not fallen into madness. Even though you were baptized with a Muslim name, it would have been better a thousand and one times to reveal yourself to the world in a less warlike context, not that you are the product of carnal Christianity, but if only to avoid the pitfalls of the analogy. This is clearly not the time to convert!

On this day after the massacre ordered by Daech, while the remains are still smoking, and candles are flickering at the edge of the windows from which hang tricolored flags at half-mast, the question of the ordinary exercise of Muslim worship in France has ignited the Web, each one making its own comment on social networks.

Thus I read a long plea published in his name in which Selim deftly enumerates pacifist suras from the Koran, sometimes in French, sometimes in Arabic, in response to critics of Islam who imagine that most Muslims are patent terrorists.

"I too can quote the Koran, except that I have read it," he boasts, with a shot of the book, bound in gold leather, open to the page of the sura known as "Al-Baqara" and tilted on a bed in front of which stands a television screen showing an episode of The *Simpsons.* "Well, well! What's this?" I thought. What's new is that Selim is a great defender of oppressed Muslims... It's madness! And since when does he know how to speak Arabic?

The son of the ogre has obviously lost his mind. My word! The national mourning has been decreed, and the gentleman is lost in useless debates, inflamed by a spirit of proselytism.

Without waiting, I went to ask him for a categorical explanation of his intervention. So that's it, it's decided?" I asked in writing, in a joking tone. When is your conversion scheduled?" There followed a long silence during which I finally caught a glimpse of the full extent of the plot. "Okay, well, I'll take your silence as a 'yes'." After recovering the use of speech, fifteen minutes later, Selim would reply, "It's already done. I've been a Muslim for almost a year."

How is this possible? Selim was chloroformed, and what else! I answered hurriedly, forgetting all about Esau:

"Why say all this now?

- I can't talk to you about it any longer on social media," he continued via text message. Anything I write here will be held against me. All my emails are subject to scrutiny, you see. People other than me have access to this account.

- Who the hell, and why? If you have any problems, you can talk to me, Selim. First, change the password!

- It's not that simple. To answer your first question, I converted once for love of Hasna, that's all," Selim justified himself.

I didn't see it coming. How could I have missed it? This is what it costs to get lost in stories and other meaningless press articles. Given your youth, Selim, you are looking for a new family, which is quite normal, because you are alone. So blinded are you by your obsessive desire to be pouponner with wish, you made of Hasna your pis-aller, what one is resigned, for lack of better. I specify, by the way, that one minute is enough to embrace Islam.

I enter a maze of crazy hypotheses, including this one: what if the story of this sudden conversion was rather that of a terrorist radicalization? Why tell me about your conversion to Islam in the middle of a state of emergency? A simple coincidence, perhaps...

From the back of my mind come back four by four certain compromising memories. Also, I don't forget that

16. Crime of apostasy

Selim had mysteriously vanished among the great lions of the Atlas Mountains, from October 15 to 23, 2014, less than a month after the beheading of Nice-based mountain guide Hervé Gourdel by AQIM terrorists. I had feared that you would be their next victim. What if, instead, you were in fact an executioner? The first reason given by the son of the ogre was his urge to go climb the Atlas mountains alone, only to admit that he was really going to meet Hasna. I am now entitled to think that it was perhaps a new alibi set up from scratch. For his part, Selim is still just as categorical on this point, even if he doesn't give much away.

Yes," he told me forcefully. I went to Algeria to meet Hasna, and to ask her parents for her hand in marriage, but I also spent three days alone up there, on the Atlas, in communion with nature, without anyone to bother me."

If religion makes you feel better, that's all that matters. It does, however, promise a serious beating.

The other big news of the day is that I managed to get my hands on the series of five black and white photos showing Esau in 1976, the same ones that the newspaper *La Provence* tried to hide from the world.

What did I see in these silver photographs? A well-combed man with a triangular face, standing frontally, then in profile, drowned in a stagnant crowd. Esau has a hard-featured, horse-like face with a rather long, pointed nose, wearing thin metal-framed glasses. With his hands on his hips, he has a bowl cut with jet hair, a light suit, and bony, shadowy, clean-shaven cheeks.

Let's speak frankly. There is no Esau here, nor Michel Fourniret in his prime. No, it's something else entirely. It seems that there is some mystery behind it. Because in truth, on these photos, I thought I saw Selim, in flesh and blood.

The "ogre of the Ardennes" at the court of Aix-en-Provence in 1976? It is extraordinary! After all, isn't he the real monster of the Etang de Berre, the one who took the life of Marie-Dolorès Rambla on June 3, 1974? Let's suppose for a moment that the Fourniret trail is proven, whatever the cops say... Was Christian Ranucci unjustly guillotined?

Agitated by these thoughts, I try to untangle the skein where the threads of both the Fourniret and Ranucci cases are intertwined. A vision appears to me, the public prosecutor Francis Nachbar, both hands crossed in front of his face: "Cover this Fourniret, that I cannot see!"

Even as I sail off into the sunset, with Colonel Mizu comfortably spread out on the sideboard, a thought comes to electrify me, annihilating all torpor in me. With a sudden leap, I rush to my office. I activate the brass and green opaline banker's lamp, then I slide from an envelope the five controversial photographs on which Esau is dancing. I pick one at random, and join it in a diptych with a portrait, more or less recent, of Michel Fourniret. Who knows, the parallelism between the image of the ogre and that of his twin brother could give a new meaning to the Ranucci case.

Why didn't I think of this earlier? From a drawer, I extract a watchmaker's magnifying glass, which I insert into my slashed eyebrow. Let's take the analogy a step further. No matter what the competent authorities have said, it is not the drooping eyebrows, nor the glasses, and even less the dimpled chin of his double that obscures Esau's hallucinatory resemblance to the Carolomacherian assassin, but rather the non-commissioned officer's goatee that he now sports, thus contrasting with the photos of the time, where he presented a hairless face. But is it a pure coincidence that Michel Fourniret had the idea to follow these hair habits and customs?

What if the key to the enigma was hidden in Michel Fourniret's uncultivated, spiky beard? For sure, Selim will be able to tell me more. No matter what time it is, if there is an emergency, I will wake him up from his sleep with a sharp voice: "Hello! Selim? This is Oli... There's no need to search any further... I've got them... You know, the photos... Yes... We're gaining ground... We've got to crack down... Yes... That's it... Perfect... 10 o'clock at the old Wobben. See you tomorrow..." Here is the dawn. At the end of my nerves, my calves sheared off, I fall on the couch on my stomach, and sink into a sleep of anvil.

That morning at the counter, here we are. "Well, here you are, my dear! So what do you say, Selim, what do you say? Are they symmetrical?", I launched, all panting, while tinkering in front of him, between two cups of steaming coffee and a carafe of chipped water, the diptych Esau/Fourniret. "But speak, say something!" Selim goes to sigh in my ear, but the cry of the wind covers his stammering similar to a snore. And then, finally...: "But... Me, Oli... I'm not blind... Him here...", he gibbers, shaking his head. "Damn, it's terrible! It's true that he looks just like him!" And... hop! A point for Belgium! Selim, if you had to bet big," I said, getting straight to the point, "which horse would you bet your money on? Would you say, in the blink of an eye, that it is Michel in his green years? "And the police, what did they conclude? "Only your opinion counts, my friend," I said, in an intentionally terse manner. "After all, this is your father we're talking about. Your word is worth a thousand times more than that of a puppet army composed of Nachbar, Judge Michel, Valéry Giscard d'Estaing, and his straw men! You've been around him long enough to determine if there is any doubt."

"So, I'll answer you: yes, it's Michel," Selim says. "No mistake, it's him. If it's not him, it's his clone. Yes, they are absolutely identical, one and the other. I know he wore his hair long like that when he was young. I will never forget his nose, but also the shape of his face. I saw that face as I see you, Oli! It is Michel. It's certain. It's unimaginable! I would cut my nose to spite my face, and I don't know what else!

Not a sound now. A very graceful squad of singing mermaids with golden scales has just appeared in the doorway of the Wobben, capturing all our attention.

"If not, tell me, what I'm going to ask you is delicate, but I have to ask the question in order to rule out any vain hypothesis. Have you ever seen Michael with a beard? No ?

- No, never, never. He let it grow at the opening of his trial in 2008. Why such a question?

- Well, what a coincidence! And how do you justify it?

- All I can tell you is that before he got caught, he never had any semblance of a beard. In fact, it was quite the opposite. He was a clean-shaven guy, every morning. He attached particular importance to being very clean. Curious idea that he had, in prison...

- But then... but then... He will have had recourse to a false beard!, I exclaimed, with enthusiasm. A trompe-l'oeil, a mask... Ah! We are on the right track!

- What do you mean? What are you saying? Are you suggesting that Michael has hidden his features under a beard to divert suspicion? Well, frankly, it's very likely, indeed, Judge Selim. Let's agree on that, but then that would mean that this Ranucci you're talking about was unjustly convicted. But... But... But that's horrible! And to think that we can't do anything... Alas!

- Sorry, Selim, but yes, there is a way... And this way, here it is... "

Let's play it straight. I grab a snapshot of Esau lying on the counter, then hand Selim a sheet of paper and a pen. "One thing to do. We'll write a little message to your father:

- I'm listening," Selim replies, glancing absent-mindedly in the direction of the young women in the room.

- That's it. Write, Selim, write these few words: "Is that you? Then I asked Selim to put his signature at the bottom of this message.

When night comes, while I am sitting in a Neapolitan restaurant along the pier of the port of Nice, with a breath-taking view of Eastern girls lounging in the mist, under the drizzle, I take out of the pocket of my anorak a pair of scissors, a stick of glue, and assemble, alongside a plate of steaming spaghetti, a blank sheet of paper where only Selim's signature appears and Esau's portrait, in such a way that they form the obverse and reverse of the same medallion. I fold the whole thing into a large brown gusseted envelope stamped with a new candy-pink postage stamp by the artist Ben Vautier, on which is written "this is an invitation", which I give to that gluttonous Pac-Man. We'll soon know.

We are hopeful that this very short letter will reach its destination without getting stuck in the wheels of the censorship committee. At first, it will be in the possession of the prison warden, or even of a second-rate psychiatrist. They are the ones who will read it, and believe me, they will never manage to make the connection between any image and a criminal case that has been closed for over forty years. If we exclude the investigators, the members of the administrative body will believe, at most, that Selim found an old photo of his father in a box.

While we are still wondering if the starving Selim is involved with the radical Islamist movement, I learn, by the greatest of coincidences, that he went to the French Blood Establishment to donate blood, only to be politely escorted out on the grounds that he had already "given too much". According to the rules, a man can donate blood up to six times a year. No doubt this is a way to absolve himself, in the eyes of others, of the vileness committed by his father and his ogressive mother... Our friend, by his generosity and his chivalrous manners, borders on sanctity. Always in search of excellence, he will even go so far as to donate bone marrow, on November 9, 2017. "On behalf of the patient who has regained hope thanks to your generosity," a representative of the medical profession wrote to him, "we want to thank you for the immense desire to live that you have given him back. A highly symbolic present will be attached to this letter of thanks: a silver hourglass set in a glass block. Some would see this as a way to save time and draw a definitive line on the vestiges of a sad past. That'll teach me! Let us blush at our prejudices and draw a favorable veil over our past mistakes. Let us not give an unjustly excessive importance to the new spiritual life of the small prince of Sautou.

On March 10, 1976, Paul Lombard, Christian Ranucci's lawyer, before the Bouches-du-Rhône Assize Court, ended his eloquent plea with these remarkable words: "Do not listen to the vile rumor. Do not listen to the public opinion that knocks on the door of this room. She is a prostitute who pulls the judge by the sleeve. She must be driven out of our courtrooms, for when she enters one door, justice leaves through the other. I don't care about public opinion.

17.
GOLD FEVER

"The journalist is the historian of the moment."
Albert Camus

December 8, 2015, in Nice

The hose connecting the radiator to the engine of my cart has just burst. While I spend a precious time, arms plunged into these viscous entrails, trying to seal the breaches, hands covered with latex, Selim announces me by phone that a letter has just arrived from the prison of Ensisheim. It must be a reaction to our October 11 firebrand. All of a sudden, a reddish oil splashes on me and mixes with my sweat. It was at this moment that Selim sent me a series of three photographs reproducing the contents of prisoner's sheet n°5451.

Curiously, the number 10 is indicated at the outset. On the next page, I read the number 11, which suggests, logically, a classification of the pages in ascending order. I hear you, my dear Fourniret... But... But that can't be... It suggests that there should be nine other pages here. If so, where are they?

"I had the same thought," admits Selim, by phone.

"It's great, his text has been redacted by the censorship committee of the central house of Ensisheim! We may have the proof here."

However, the first words of Michel Fourniret's manuscript are consistent with a classic introduction. The heading reads: "To Selim, Gwenhaël, Jean-Pierre". What if it was a coded message intended not to be understood by members of the "Interior Party"[20] ? "It's very likely," says Selim, on the other end of the line. In this case, what can the numbers 10 and 11 mean, when aligned on the same grid line? Several combinations are possible in the latter case, such as, for example, the eternal Holy Trinity, transfigured by the number 3. Indeed, if we start from the principle that 10 + 11 give 21, and then I add the two digits of this number as simple units in the form of 2 + 1, then it gives 3, right? Ditto for the sequence of numbers 10 and 11, which in turn can be rethought as 1 + 0 + 1 + 1 = 3.

Michel Fourniret, *to Selim* - Although perfidious adviser, far from being vain, is my anger! Lady! If it makes us angry, it allows us to exclaim: "Pff! too stupid! Less than a drum, Selim reasons. A sign that his neurons are working? As for their impulsiveness? Well, not really. Well, everyone has their own cup of tea. Therefore?

***

---

20. Reference to the anticipation novel *1984* by George Orwell, published in 1949. The Inner Party is the name given to the ruling class.

I believe that the adverb of time "therefore" is a homophone of the sentence "gold". These words share, except for one detail, the same pronunciation. "Less than a drum, Selim reasons". Is the ogre implying that his dirty money was stashed in the drum of a washing machine? It is worth quoting an article from Le *Parisien* of April 29, 2005, entitled "Fourniret's mysterious booty", in which it is said that "Fourniret would have taken only 20 kilos of gold that were quickly resold in a numismatic agency in Brussels, the rest of this fortune being destined for Hellegouarch. A hundred napoleons were placed in the *drum of a washing machine* [italics added] in Sart-Custinne. In conclusion, the journalist François Vignolle specifies - and this is really not trivial - that "the search in good standing carried out at Fourniret's home did not yield anything". Is this a sign that we are on the right track to make us rich, or am I fit for the asylum?

Michel Fourniret. - Seeing his old man as a stranger? Biped with a deranged brain? This, from behind opaque glasses, via casual eyes? It is your right. Yes, it is your right to dare to look at him. Even if it means leaving him dumbfounded. A guy who, having arrived as a virgin, is not a little proud of his demands. Innocence! In front of the mayor of Vrigne-aux-Bois.

***

In response to the announcement of Selim's matrimonial project with a person he knows absolutely nothing about, Fourniret, inside a thick cloud of fog scribbled in green pencil, makes a violent indictment of women who do not arrive at the wedding as virgins. This is a very curious way to congratulate her boy. Obviously, the Ardennais refers here, not without vivacity, to his first wife, Annette Rennesson, married in 1963. He could never get used to the idea of having been deprived of his right to marry her. These are precisely the reasons that he alleges to justify his hunt for non-virgins.

Michel Fourniret. - Marieur of a lady "remainders of the others" to the most backward of the apostles, was certainly enough silly to marry the "crane to the barks". That, by way of letter! When Annette confessed to me that she had already had a relationship, the world fell apart, it became a pile of shit. My pride was hit hard.

Decidedly, the ogre is always so spiritual!

Michel Fourniret. - Algiers - Oued-Smar - Oued Barek - Sedan. Bremgarlen. Air Commando - Sedan.

Why does the "ogre of the Ardennes" suddenly evoke Algeria? There is no doubt that he is referring to Hasna, with whom Selim was to marry until fate dictated otherwise. It is obvious. But how did he know, from his cell in Alsace, that the infidel was of Algerian nationality? Never was there any mention, in our writings, of Algeria. The convoluted confession of Michel Fourniret is clear, formal, and therefore defiant. How was this information brought to his attention? Faced with the doubts that arise, I call Selim at full speed. He is stunned: "Oh, I don't know," he answers, a little bit stung. Take my word for it, Oli, I was just as surprised as you were. Anyway, he can say whatever he wants. I don't care. No doubt Michael has asked someone to spy on me..."

So I repressed, with great difficulty, my desire to share with him my well-founded worries. I know the son of the ogre is very fragile, despite his debonair airs. It is nevertheless true that we are being watched. That a convict can draw around him sentinels who have agreed to act on his behalf beyond the bars, thus making any ubiquitous feat possible, is highly probable. Of course, it seems quite insane to order exactions and assassinations from purgatory, but this has been seen before.

Consider the case of Lynette Fromme. On September 5, 1975, in Sacramento, this hippie with a face like an angel tried to put a hole in the skin of the thirty-eighth president of the United States on the orders of the guru Charles Manson, who was imprisoned for a series of seven murders committed by his followers, without ever getting his hands dirty. Michel Fourniret, he is there, he is looking at us through the murder holes of the Ensisheim power plant...

Very good! But, that still doesn't tell us what the combination "Algiers - Oued-Smar - Oued Barek → Sedan" can mean. Algiers is the capital of Algeria. Oued-Smar is a commune of the *wilaya* located in the eastern suburbs of Algiers. Finally, Oued Barek happens to be a river, flowing south. For the sake of clarity, I draw the projections of the lines Fourniret mentions on a map of Algeria, pinned on a cork board above my desk in the alcove. Once connected, they reveal nothing conclusive, nothing except a triangle with unequal sides similar to a delta radiating out and converging on Sedan, where Fourniret was born. Some will object that this is making too much of the ravings of a mental defective, never at the end of his trivia. They will be right.

Michel Fourniret, *to Selim* - Yes! It's your right to have a forehead, to have so little in the lemon, that you'll laugh at me when you read this letter. Which idiot - he had to be a coward! - will show up in front of Saint Peter, no less hilarious than the Madonna! Without popol = his little rapier having ever denied anyone! The naive candor, it is a pity, is not an Olympic discipline. Your old man ? Right away a gold medalist.

***

May Their Graces do me the honor of seeing, as I see it, this proud Ardennais brandishing the inscription "GOLD" in capital letters dashing here like a victorious fist gloved in white. Everything here is articulated and disarticulated around this word "gold". Without doubt it is the only thing worth reading, precisely because it puts us on the track of the fabulous treasure, which he seems to consider as an Olympic trophy.

Michel Fourniret. - Since the dawn of time, Mother Nature (Allah = kif-kif), never did, never does anything without reason. Never! Wherever it is in the universe, since the pure heart of the primate, of the caveman without futal, nor suit and tie, Mr. Neandertal = constant regeneration. Galloping acculturation. Our fathers ? They saw the horizon from the bottom of a well. From now on ? Out of the horizon telly ? Lobotomized empty heads. Yuck!

How! This vile hanger-on Fourniret goes about talking Arabic, without any apparent motive, to the point of pronouncing the name of God in all those who profess Mohammedanism. Why now, precisely? There is a glaring irony, of course, because finally the reference to this religion is inappropriate in this matter. On the one hand, the prisoner n° 5451 is absolutely not supposed to know about the announcement of Selim's conversion to Islam. On the other hand, this is the first time he has spoken in Arabic. Henceforth, the doubt is not allowed any more. For me, Michel Fourniret managed to be put in the perfume, that it is for Hasna, or the new devotion of his son to Allah. In the confusion, these words of Fourniret, pronounced during the hearing in 2008, come back to my mind: "If extraterrestrials followed the trial, it must have made them say that there are gifted people among the earthlings".

On the other hand, these winks to the Muslim world are neither more nor less than the logical consequences of the media hype, of which we are all victims to some extent. No doubt Fourniret keeps himself informed by reading the newspapers or watching TV. Islam... Currently, the headlines of the news are devoted only to Islam! Everywhere, it's all they talk about!

But doesn't the disavowed monarch repeat, by his own admission, that "Mother Nature never did anything without reason"? Yes, but what are we to believe of a pedophile murderer who constantly amuses himself by leading the investigators astray towards false leads?

Michel Fourniret. - Your mail mailed on October 27, 2015, if it was opened upon receipt by the administration department, then closed with a staple after. Regulatory reading, before being handed to me?

✳✳✳

Big Brother watches over us with his squinting eye, scrutinizing everything we write. Indeed, Selim and I have never sealed a ballot with any staple. What Michel Fourniret wants above all is to invite him, by means of a tacit agreement, to the strictest vigilance, which would not be possible without the use of a language codified around common objectives.

Next time, we will redouble our efforts, if there is a next time, because finally, in the last lines of his letter, the ogre of the Ardennes, in response to the jousting of the spirit, uses the threat to force his son to submit to his omnipotence, failing which he will dedicate him to everything. The writing, at first straight and regular, suddenly becomes anarchic over the pages.

Michel Fourniret. - To this day, I still do not know the content of your last letter. Your ostensible [missing word] dissuaded me from reading it. My observation: a mega chasm separates a father from his youngest son. Are you getting your claws out? Fine, it's your choice. Just as it is my right to keep his reading under wraps. Waiting. Waiting for what? Who knows? To come and see me? I'm free not to leave my thebaid - even if it's only an inch. Even if someone comes to me, with the courtesy of 95% of the prison officers, and says: *"You have a visitor"*.

Conclusion: water will have to flow long, long, long, long under the bridge before I agree to go to the field where your impersonal way of seeing things is. I will not leave my cell or my yard. Is that it? Is it clear in your mind? Very clear?

This being passed, if it happens that one day resurrected, my son Selim ? For the time being, a bistro pillar? That the aforementioned younger son renounces his visible complacency to mediocrity? Recover his legitimate pride? His old man will die without ever - the ultimate for a guy who arrived at the wedding as a virgin, and not a little proud to distinguish himself from other guys without pride - having denounced anyone.

If you happen to want to see, as a visitor, some centers, and this, moved by the same curiosity as those of the visitors of the zoo of Vincennes, where each one throws to the monkeys some peanuts, well, visit your mother in detention. Consequently, I suspend my doodling shipments to Vallauris. Message over.

P.S.: I had to bark! I had to get it out! Hi.

***

Unfortunate news for us, pirates of junk who sail at low tide, in search of gold. Damn Fourniret! Grave robber! Here he comes to threaten Selim not to unseal the letters sealed with his seal, experienced in all the tricks of cowardice, and huddled behind a barricade of monologues. The disavowed monarch, who is a stickler for principles, intends to teach what it costs to unleash the mockery on him, a game we play all the more willingly when there is no fatal danger.

"There, you see, sighs the prince of Sautou in the handset, the throat burning, it starts seriously to break me menu, the old man! It's heating me up! How dare he?

- Perhaps we went too far, too fast. We have been hammering him relentlessly for almost two years, the better to wear him down and erode him, cornered in the ropes. If you ask me, we have no choice but to give in to his carabinerous blackmail.

- I'm tired of your bullshit, okay? he yells.

- Let's see Selim! After all, you have to be diplomatic once in a while..."

In a moment, a tumult of swallowing rises at the other end of the line. A few seconds later, the huge uproar ends after several jerks. The line is cut.

Selim just hung up on me. I am not unaware of his deep malaise. The most serious thing is the ultimate consequences of Michel Fourniret's choice to let our letters turn yellow at the bottom of a vase. For if he carries out his threats, thus putting an end to our epistolary exchanges, rich in more than a hundred letters, what will happen to the treasure? And will the question of whether Esau is really the devil incarnate of Fourniret remain unanswered?

If we wish so much to call her father back to propriety, and to redeploy our game without great risk, we must first make amends without insulting him, and fall, however ridiculous it may seem, into sycophancy. This is in practice its only fuel. In 2008, Nicole, Michel Fourniret's second wife, confided this herself in the witness box, as reported in the *Journal du dimanche* of March 30, 2008: "He is a great manipulator. He likes to force people to do what he wants. He is a character of inordinate pride that pushes him to extreme limits."

Suddenly, my cell phone, in the back pocket of my pants, starts to vibrate. A message has just fallen.

Selim, *by SMS* - I talked to my boss to get two days off in January. We have to make good use of the visit permit that was given to us. So, we're going to see this coward in prison, in Ensisheim, and give him the beating he deserves. When do we leave? You're the brain. Let me know so I can make the best arrangements.

***

Early in the morning, I salute on my knees the illustrious colonel Mizu, position of the hands in triangle. Untied, shoulders and elbows disarticulated, I put on over my pyjamas a black silk kimono edged with red, embroidered with a Rozan dragon, then reach the olive garden under a row of green arches, telephone in hand. In spite of the wind's bites, the branches, blued by the cold, remain stoic, numb, as if they had been condemned to the torture of the withers. It is polar cold. I grabbed the phone and dialed the number of the central prison in Ensisheim. I barely swallowed a hot sip of coffee:

"Hello, yes, I'm listening...

- Hello, hello, sir, am I at the central house of Ensisheim?

- Yeah, that's right, sir! confirms the operator in his own way.

- I would like to make an appointment to visit the visiting room. A visit permit has been issued to me for this purpose by your director.

- Who's it for, sir, if you want to?

- The prisoner n° 5451.

- I need a name, sir," he continued, in the same monotone.

- F... Fourniret ! It's for Michel Fourniret, I stammered, dumbfounded, so much the concretization of a meeting with this sawyer of cross seems unreal to me.

- Okay, but you're... you're...

- I am only a simple companion, a moral crutch, in a way, for his son, Selim.

- I see. And, when do you plan to come here?"

Visiting Michel Fourniret in prison... Ah! terrible project that one, and of which I weigh all the danger only when I am on the point of concretizing it...

"Hello?" the prison switchboard operator, still on the line, gets impatient. Come on, come on! I need to have some nerve, and to draw all my courage from the weight of the civic prescriptions of the *mos maiorum*, model of Roman morals under the Empire. The party is taken, without possible contest. I determine the exact time at which Selim must collide with Michel Fourniret.

It's official. The last-born of Monique Olivier's brood - the "culot", as the peasants say - will appear before its creator in Ensisheim, on January 16, 2016, from 10:15 am to 11:45 am, that is to say in one month. Having completed the preparations, all that remains is to inform him of the day of our departure. Suddenly, a question crosses my mind as I hang up the phone. What will happen to us if, in Alsace, his lordship Fourniret has such a tenacious grudge that he refuses to come to us? The answer from the switchboard operator at the central station is lapidary: "If the prisoner has no desire to see you, that is his strict right. We cannot force him to do so. It will be up to him to decide at the appropriate time.

This Fourniret pirate is always one step ahead. It is very likely that we incur expenses for nothing. If my memory does not betray me, Michel Fourniret has, moreover, forbidden Selim to set foot in the bush. To hell with our fears! For sure, he will come. It's been twelve years since this bilge rat has received a single visit. It would be absurd to suppose that he is reluctant to leave his dingy hole... He needs an audience only too much to feel he exists. His need to be flattered is far too great. Selim is all he has left. Selim is the key. Only he can stand up to his rantings.

18.

SELIM THE FREEDMAN

> "If a grain of passion enters the heart,
> It enters a grain of possible fiasco."
> Stendhal

December 23, 2015, in Nice

Selim, bearded, makes a remarkable entrance at the old Wobben. He twists his nose on the lentils while spouting a string of insults, both elbows planted on the table, cuffs unbuttoned. Confident in his devotion, he now refuses to drink any alcoholic beverage. A few days before Christmas, we occupy a table for four people, as much for our convenience as for discretion. Nothing exciting. He and I have not yet exchanged a word. I had not seen the Prince of Sautou since his lightning conversion to Islam.

An eloquent silence follows my clearing of the throat, so much so that I feel obliged to add this idle question: "Say Selim, have you prepared your list for Santa Claus? As he struggles in his too short jacket, he recovers the use of speech.

"Nothing has changed," he replies, puffed up with pride, with a sort of resentment. The super KTM 690 SMC R or nothing: 15,000 euros, my friend! Besides, what do I gain in all this story?

- Ah, money, always money!" I hammered, for lack of patience, while pretending to smell the sea air. "You only have that word in your mouth. Money! You talk to me about it as if you didn't have any, even after having gorged yourself, without flinching, on the pedophile's money orders! Do I have to remind you of the amount of the last check signed by the ogre? 500 euros! This money should normally be used to pay damages to the families of the victims, but you continue to collect his money, as if it were royalties. What the hell! You're not John Lennon's son, I know that.

Selim, then, pricks a blush. Guided by old reflexes, he busies himself, pestering between leather and flesh, throwing very significant black looks at young passers-by, on the grounds that they are too short dressed for the season. "If they are ever raped, we should not complain, and look for a culprit," he ruminates with a clear air. In pathetic moments, his fulmination is interspersed with lively looks of lust.

"None of that, Selim! Will you stop? Where are your reserved habits in society?" And then, a beer helping, Selim relaxes, and very quickly the reconciliation is sealed:

- If I'm pissed off, it's because of my co-worker, Mamadou. Like me, he is a security guard at the hardware store, but today he was late, as usual. He didn't arrive at the depot until 3 p.m., and I had to work three hours of overtime.

- And you, I suppose, felt compelled to cover for him with your boss.

- So, No! I warned Mamadou that I was going to spill the beans to Thomas, our big shot. Which I did, by demanding to be paid for my overtime. Finally, he exclaims, all smiles, Mamadou was fired. No one steps on my toes with impunity anymore! He learned that the hard way.

Father Selim has thrown away his cassock. What a surprise! At the time I knew him, he had just been swindled by Marcello, his supposed best friend. For almost a year, this Marcello had sublet a room in a sordid street in the Old Port. Every month, this rascal invented a pretext to increase his rent abusively, pretending to carry out the orders of a landlady straight out of his imagination. The good pear has thus matured.

Very quickly, our discussion refocuses on this mysterious Thomas, a young man of thirty-two whom Selim describes in very complimentary terms. Aside from Mamadou," he says, shaking the white tablecloth bordered with a red border, "I took the opportunity to ask him for permission to be away from January 15 to 17. He gave me the green light.

- Ah, you and Thomas seem to get along pretty well.

- We have a lot in common. I like to warn you right away, you won't believe your ears." Dreading the worst, I order a glass of lightly ambered rum, without ice, and empty it in one gulp in silent supplication. "If Thomas did not see any disadvantage to grant me this leave, continues the prince of Sautou, on the other hand, he required explanations. I could not see myself lying to him, so I... Well! I mentioned the town of Ensisheim, in Alsace..."

Prostrate, I beg the friendly tattooed waitress to pour me a shot of her Filipino rum. Something tells me I'm going to need it. "When Thomas heard the snoring name Ensisheim, he made big eyes at me and said: "Something tells me that you're going to 49, rue de la Première Armée française, right?", he reconstructs with a real concern for imitation, despite a bad cold. "Damn! the jerk ... I swear, I had a cold in my back!" The 49 rue de la Première Armée française corresponds very precisely to the location of the Ensisheim prison. But how did this Thomas know?

"You've been sitting at the table, haven't you? You've spilled the beans about the treasure, just say it!", I burst out, head under water, pulling him to me by the hemmed sleeve of his sweater. Yet Selim is adamant about this.

No, no, no and no!" he hammers, his right hand raised.

- There is a traitor among us. In any case, if someone has tipped off the Parisians, we are done for. In addition to having our chestnuts pulled out of the fire, we'll soon be used as game. Do I have to remind you that I have been registered with the police? The prince of Sautou, after listening to me ramble for several minutes during which I did not stop agonizing him, swerves. "No, you are not there at all ", he cuts me, by opposing me an embarrassed refusal, followed by a grimace of his own which would make him pass unnoticed among the Moaï. "You know, sometimes I think you should really stop making movies, especially your old gangster movies. It makes you completely paranoid. Selim has a point. I nod gently, "I'm listening."

After closing the door behind him, Thomas confessed to Selim: "I too often go to 49 rue de la Première Armée française. My father has lived there since 2007. This led Selim to ask:

"Ah, your father is in the prison guard?

- No, he wanted to cool my mother off."

His answer left Selim stunned. That two perfect quidams, each with an outlaw for a father detained in the shadow of the walls of the same prison, 700 kilometers from Nice, could find themselves working together, by chance, in the same company, is not without salt! What a singular duo! All this is much too big to be a simple coincidence. Frankly, do you know many sons of convicts detained in Ensisheim? Stung to the core, Thomas then let himself go to curiosity.

- "And you, Selim, who are you going to visit behind bars?

- Me too, you see, I'm going to visit my father. The only difference - and it's a big one - is that mine got life. The exact term is life imprisonment. Michel Fourniret, does that mean anything to you?

Flabbergasted, Thomas *at* first thought it was a joke. When he realized who was in front of him, the poor guy turned so pale that he looked like he had just seen a screaming ghost, dressed as a clown, waving his chains over his shaved head. "He thought he was the most to be pitied," Selim laughed, holding his ribs.

Even with the best will in the world, I would never have the mind to invent such a bloody complicated story. At first glance, it's impossible not to see the mark of fate. Unless the ogre's son is a fantastic invention of my subconscious. Besides, something tells me that Selim and Thomas will soon become the best of friends. "Having been raised by a scoundrel, it creates bonds", Selim ironically says, and for once he manages to get a smile out of me, albeit a tense one, but oh so sincere.

But wait a minute... Now that I think about it... Suddenly, my natural distrust goes up several notches. My heart races. There! I'm there... What if the famous mole - whose existence I still suspect - was none other than Thomas? It would not be surprising. Selim - as we have seen - almost always ends up being fooled by those he likes, and who in reality play him Machiavellianly, as if he were a common commodity. It is useless, therefore, to blame fate.

Let us judge by analogy: it could be, indeed, that Thomas obeyed an order by infiltrating the hardware store within the framework of a spying mission ordered by Fourniret. Moreover, if this were to prove true, it would explain many things, such as how Fourniret could be so well informed about events in the outside world. O Thomas, would you be one of those traitors?

***

The next day, in another heated letter, Michel Fourniret cleared up any misunderstanding. He served me on a platter the irrefutable proof of the existence of a mole by attaching to his prose an Epinal picture representing Christ carrying the heavy cross on his bruised shoulders. So far nothing unusual, except that this vignette has been sorely crossed out with a cobalt blue pencil. Above the Redeemer is a halo marked with the word "useless". And also: "Hairpiece and beard of ayatollah? To scare the citizens. It's not a Christian confession! I think it prays to Allah.

There is no need, in my opinion, to dwell on the coincidences that coagulate around the Prince of Sautou. On closer inspection, it is likely that the serial killer is not involved in the religious upbringing of his son. Let's not fool ourselves any more, in any way! It should be noted that Michel Fourniret, himself, used to repeat: "Mother Nature never says, never does anything without a reason." This is, by far, the most used phrase, more than thirty occurrences! Let's reject all imposture!

Michel Fourniret intends to make it clear that he is perfectly aware of his son's evolution, which includes his conversion to Islam. I realize that his references to current events are all the more meaningful as they are part of a larger process, which he takes advantage of here to make it clear that he is the one who is manipulating us, and not the other way around... The hardware store that employs Selim is nothing but a den of spies and collaborators of the pedophile, where everyone is plotting!

If all this remains to be proven, here's how I see things: cunning, Thomas manages to gather a maximum of information on Selim's account, entrusts it to his father, Alain, during visits to the visiting room, who then hastens to repeat it all to Michel Fourniret in the courtyard, with an interested counterparty in mind, money, or what else? Foodstuffs? Given his less than stellar background, I am tempted to believe it. Anyway, I am careful not to tell Selim about this theory, fearing to spoil a budding friendship unnecessarily, in case my theory is wrong. And anyway, he would not understand, would feel attacked, I know it. He would repeat that Thomas is an honest man, not at all in the pay of the enemy, and then forbid me even to suspect him...

***

I have to admit that I'm happy for Selim, who has always had such a hard time making sincere friendships because of his genetic code. Here is a story he told me recently.

Selim once counted among his close friends a man named Hugues, whose family lived in Sart-Custinne at the same time as the Fournirets. These two were not in the same class, but they were very close. It was the time of innocence, of bowl cuts, of Brazilian jiu-jitsu classes... It so happens that three years ago - by an incredible chance - this native of

18. Selim the freedman

Charleroi came to settle, in his turn, in the Alpes-Maritimes department, in Mandelieu-la-Napoule, near Cannes, that is to say twenty minutes away from the place where Selim, his childhood friend, used to live

I hadn't seen Hugues since the affair broke in 2003," he said. When the police neutralized Mich-Mich, who was immediately thrown into prison, my mother and I left Sart-Custinne without telling anyone. Afterwards, I knew that he had come to live near here. I was looking forward to seeing him again. So I expressed my desire to see him again, but it was not shared. And that is understandable!"

Hugues, in response to his resumption of contact via social networks, let him know, without bluntness or diplomacy, that he preferred to cut the bridges, the crimes of his creator forming "the unbreakable horizon of their friendship". What a sadness! I feel so much sorrow to tell this memory. When one day, I allowed myself to ask for explanations to this boy, via Internet, he started at the quarter turn, not drying up of praises on the "ogre of the Ardennes", whom he knew well, thus circumventing the question on Selim, of which he obviously does not care.

Apart from the unheard of crimes he committed," he wrote to me, "although that was not the point, Michel Fourniret was an excellent construction professional. He had golden hands like no other, and knew a lot about the different building trades, whether in masonry, plumbing, or electricity or electronics."

***

Come on, now we have to start writing a letter, in response to the pressure exerted by Fourniret. The last

I heard, he was threatening to suspend all epistolary relations, indignant at the idea that Selim could raise the note by half a tone, and thus upset patriarchal values. Among the Fournirets, partisans of organized chaos, one does not trifle with the absolute primacy of the father over the son. Maybe he's bluffing... He invents a life to appear strong. Nevertheless, if we want to try to overthrow the throne of Sautou, I suggest that we flatten ourselves, and show our hands for the very last time.

Between two rounds of beer, I tell Selim why I think it is highly desirable to conclude a non-aggression pact. We must be very patient. He accepts, but under the express condition that he does not use a vulgar sheet of paper. Let it be! Selim plunges his hand into the zipper of his bag with zipped compartments, rummages around on the left and on the right, and pulls out, with majesty, a block of squared paper, impeccably stacked, and a box of colors.

In a flash, he starts to scribble a sign on the full page with an explanatory note that reads: "White Flag". How about that! A clever way to loosen the grip.

Selim, *to Michel Fourniret* - Oh, it's okay! Don't be a sissy. No fuss between us. Say Mich-Mich, a journalist claims that you suffer from Parkinson's disease. Is that true, are you sick? Do you have any special medical treatment?

Why these sudden allusions to Algeria in your last letter? What is the connection between this exotic folklore and me? I don't see the connection. In any case, if it happens that this Muraille writes to you, know that he is lying about everything. Do not answer him under any circumstances. Please spare me any "media hype", to use your expression. It's hard enough as it is. I beg you to spare me the same fate as Marie-Hélène, who died following a drug overdose on February 21, 2006.

By the way, I have never used any kind of ornament to seal a letter. No staples. The censorship committee is watching us. It watches us, it watches us...

P.S.: What did you think of the portrait of you that I sent you? Did you like to see this old photo from your youth?

***

Once the letter is finished, I examine the document with my naked eye. By my faith! It is the work of a maniac. The calligraphy is perfect. The letters, elegant and ornate, are drawn with infinite delicacy. Each line is straight, as if drawn with a ruler. No matter how hard I look, I cannot see any ink smudges or pencil marks on the paper. I am inclined to believe that Selim wishes to give his father the image of a disciplined pupil unjustly delivered to slander, and beset by doubts. It is then that I understand, in proportion, that I only have to stamp his little masterpiece to fly back home. When all of a sudden, he calls me while rolling up his sleeves, like a magician getting ready to reveal the secrets of his sleight of hand: "Hey, by the way, your treasure story," he says, as terse as he is cryptic, "what makes you say that a part of it is always buried there, somewhere, in a crevice?

I have a bad feeling about this.

"Alas! My poor Oli," he declaimed emphatically. Learn, and this without offence, that the share of the booty which went to my mother after the arrest of Mich-Mich has been completely consumed. What is the use of being so foolishly obstinate?"

What is he trying to say? Wiggling my nose, my moustache is suddenly clogged with a brackish water, which I immediately interpret as the adulterated foretaste of the bitter failure of my chimerical, if not downright comic, quest.

My mother... Bah!" energetically launches the son of the "ogre of the Ardennes", wrapping his hand around her neck. His share of the Postiches' treasure... Bah! There's nothing left of it! well, I think!

- How do you know?" I asked abruptly, mopping my forehead with my sleeve. "How can you be so sure? Come on, explain yourself."

Selim sneers: "It was I who buried the gold. Selim Fourniret? Bloody phony! Since all this time, he would have dared to lead me on a boat, knowing full well that it would lead nowhere? Judas ! I would have run for two years after a vulgar chimera?

"Fourniret ! Fourniret! You're saying revolting things to me. Our plans have been in place for weeks. If you knew that in advance, why are you telling me now? Out of calculation? Answer me! Why? Look at me. Selim.

- No, no. Maybe it's you who didn't know how to read between the lines," Selim stammers, muttering a confused confession. Is it possible that you are also deaf?

- Fourniret, you lie!

- I'm telling you, Oli...

- Is this a joke?"

Look at him! Proud of provoking this stampede, he confesses his lie to me with a smile at the corner of his lips, and without apology. Vile swindler of Ardennes! This insolent... I had innocently trusted him... and he...

If the prince of Sautou held this language with the nose and the beard of the Postiches, he would be roasted with

18. Selim the freedman

a cane in the second which follows, without warning, nor hesitation. Let them strangle you! Drown him, Postiches! Drown him! Impale him! If I listened to myself, I would go and flay you alive, you buffoon of the wren!

No! No! Let's calm down... Anger is a bad advisor. To fall into the prince's disgrace would be a disaster, a fault... And yet, everything seems to be conspiring to break the understanding between us. I find it hard to take the news. Coolness! In any case, I assure you, Selim, that I will not risk a thousand deaths for you anymore. At that, I burst out laughing nervously, picked up my coffee-stand and emptied it in one go! Full of despair, I greet the Fourniret son with a barely veiled cynical gesture, and leave the camp in a gust of wind, disgusted with this whole masquerade.

Oh! the treasure of the Postiches... This sweet chimera buried, vanished... It is not so much to see my chances of making fortune destroyed that is sad to cry, as to understand that I failed. Proud investigator, I had so much faith in my abilities that I convinced myself that I knew how to squeeze the wind, when in reality I had crushed my nose against a frame lined with painted canvas.

In spite of the rebuff, I am, in a way that defies reason, ravaged by a deep pity for the son of the ogre. In this regard, I share the opinion of my mother, Nunziata, who maintains, with her customary kindness, that Selim is in a position to receive the grace of forgiveness acquired at the Cross, given his background. You see, he needed a friendly shoulder to cry on without restraint, thus granting himself the unheard-of luxury of no longer being alone. It's no wonder that one who has been abandoned by all longs to be adopted. If he had told me the truth from the start, our friendship would have been nipped in the bud. No doubt he needed a sincere and devoted friend, and having sniffed out an opportunity, it had to fall on me. Of course, I'm not a psychiatrist or a social worker, but still...

***

It is fitting that I report to you here Selim Fourniret's rambling recollections about the geode full of gold, buried underground by order of the infamous Monique Olivier. You will find below a short first-person account elucidating some of the most mysterious questions of my charitable adventure.

One night, knowing that he was providing security at a home for the aging disabled, I worked him over the phone, taking advantage of the fact that he was being paid to do nothing but feed a wriggling golden cyprin. I had to tell him to consult his memory more than he should have. Although three times he pretended to remember only obscure details, a drawbridge finally came down, offering a clear view of his lost Wallonia, and all the past came back to him, awakening his fear. A bitter task! The result is an untold story that he has, so to speak, never told to anyone, least of all the police.

Selim's story

Let's go back a bit. It was more than ten years ago, and some of the details may be lost to my memory. Even worse, even if I went back, I am not sure I could find the exact location of the hoard's burial. Not that it's a trivial thing to bury a war treasure stolen from dangerous pirates, but... memory fails, you see. Anyway, here's my secret.

It was in the summer of 2003, a few months after Mich-Mich's arrest, who was then detained in the Dinant prison.

"Mother and I had just moved into a two-room apartment at 10 rue de Meuse in Waulsort, a quiet village at the eastern end of Dinant, in the province of Namur. It was a unique opportunity to start anew. But for her, it was mostly a matter of convenience to go and see "the other" in a carriage. Yet, she was still free, but she had no idea what was about to fall on her face. She didn't look stressed, though... What about the loot? Don't get impatient, I'm coming to that...

It was the vacations. On a beautiful morning in July, "Mother" asked me to put our dog Flicka on a leash and to wait for her on the porch. I now understand that this was only a pretext to hide another purpose: to cross the water to reach the King's Wood. By the way, let me tell you a little about Flicka...

Flicka was a beautiful golden retriever with blond hair. I loved my dog. Before her, there was Méli, a female Bouvier des Flandres. One day, she thought it would be a good idea to get rid of her scorched chains and go and offer herself, with all four irons in the air, to the neighbor's German shepherd, whose name was - hold on to your hat - Bandit. Their unique embrace gave life to Alf, the same year I was born in 1988.

It was only after Alf's death, at the age of fourteen, that Flicka was born. Oh, my poor Flicka... To this day, I don't know what the chickens did to her. Ah, poor Flicka... I'll never know, but I suppose you must have died a long time ago... Poor thing. Don't worry, and don't be afraid, I'll be brief on the subject. The fact is that a lot of literature has been devoted to our history. It rarely conforms to reality. Many suspicions have, in fact, been presented as proven facts. If I go out of my way, it is precisely to denounce the lies that have been written in a hurry in many a torchbearer, by some unscrupulous journalists. Here is the kind of nonsense that has been pouring down on me in hordes:

"For a meal that she did not finish, Michel Fourniret hung his daughter with a rope on the doghouse [...] He always needed to make this kind of scene to show his authority, to punish or to reward [...] The last sufferer of Michel Fourniret's blended family is called Selim. His father imposes war games on him that are not appropriate for his age. On days when there is no school, the neighbors are amazed to see the dog training sessions that Selim is involved in. The father harnesses his son with leather armbands, and throws the dog at him, sinking its fangs into his waders [...]. On other occasions, Selim is locked in a barrel that Fourniret rolls up and hides in a corner of the garden so that the dog can find him [...]. From the 2000s, Michel Fourniret was cut off from the world, he had become completely unpredictable. Once, a neighbor was shocked by the violence with which he beat his dog. He grabbed Lyka's head to smash it repeatedly on the ground [...] The animal, too aggressive with passersby, would be shot by Fourniret, and buried in the garden."

It's all wrong. From beginning to end, it's all bullshit! There wasn't even a niche in the house! Some people are really ready to invent anything to sell a paper. All this is deplorable, especially since they will answer, in order to defend themselves, and in a very formal tone, that I am hiding the past, that my memory is selective... Bullshit! Fucking assholes! Michel, as stupid as he may be, has never tied my sister to any niche. And, he never put me in a protection for the needs of a violent training, nor even locked me in a barrel. No, he didn't kill Alf between the pillars of the garden fence either. I would have remembered if he had. But... where do they get all this? The poor thing died of old age. By the way, I read somewhere that scientists have determined that "the average life span of a dog is thirteen years, taking all breeds into account".

Let's get back to the Postiches' treasure. So I was telling you that Mother and I had gone for a walk with the dog along the Meuse. On the way, Mother finally told me the real reason for this morning excursion to the King's Wood. It was to find a secluded place to put the gold safely away from prying eyes. In July 2003, our house in Sart-Custinne had been pillaged. I assure you, it was a real carnage!

On this subject, I give here knowledge of a letter of Mich-Mich addressed to his first wife, and of which I had a copy. It was written in the prison of Châlons-en-Champagne, on November 30, 2007.

Mich-Mich, *to Nicole* - This emptying will be complicated to the point that - the arms will fall to the most valiant of the movers - due to the fact that, the places, having given to the savagery of the diggers the occasion to surpass itself free of charge, the state of the second Verdun of after the battle precariousizes any displacement of who has the hardihood to risk his steps to straddle trenches! Another detail, as frightening as it is dissuasive: all the furniture on the first floor was ruthlessly piled up in the kitchen, the only place that escaped the jackhammer because of its dilapidated tiles. I would be a little less upset if a large part of the furniture did not come from Clairefontaine, and not only from Paincourt, but from the heritage of previous generations. A heritage which, in the past, was mostly preserved at Les Maisons-Blanches. The fact that I am no longer here to roll up my sleeves certainly does not help matters.

The searches in Sart-Custinne having been useless, "Mother" feared, with good reason, that the police would one day come to Waulsort to get hold of the gold that we kept preciously in the apartment.

To access the thick, unthinned forest called "King's Wood", we first had to cross the river. A very ordinary hike. To reach this point, we had to pass by the Waulsort island, located in the bed of the Meuse, where teal were floating peacefully on the surface of the yellowish water. We then took a 124-meter long wire mesh footbridge just above the Hastière dam. Once on the other side, we continued to walk along the towpath for a few dozen meters, heading west. And then we entered the virgin forest, through a chicane entrance, right in the middle of the woods, thus leaving the abrasive asphalt for the soft nature, under the cover of giant fir trees.

After five minutes spent through the ferns, we stopped on a stony slope, bordered by rocky slopes all covered with ivy. Around us, there was nothing but a field. I know the media have mentioned the ruins of Château-Thierry, but I have not seen anything like it around here. In the tall grass, the maples were rarer, and they gave way to hornbeams, oaks, lindens, and birches. Suddenly, "Mother", in a velvet jacket, held up a large black canvas purse filled with gold nuggets, and threw it at my feet. In a quavering voice, she begged me to determine where to dig. Of course, I knew what was inside, but I, like an automaton, executed promptly, almost without thinking, nor asking questions. That's how it was back then.

After some hesitation, it was agreed to dig under a hollow sycamore tree trunk, uprooted, and lying across, whose dead wood was four, or five meters long. Higher up, there was this musical thrush that played the same three notes all day long: "Tchic, tchic, tchic!" With a steady hand, I grabbed a split ash branch with torn bark, and used it to drill a fifty

18. Selim the freedman

centimeter deep hole in a bed of moss. From the weight of the bag, it was more than enough. There really wasn't much inside. Hop and hop! And so the loot vanished, under the gnarled branches of the Waulsort thicket. Finally, I planted the stick firmly and upright on the ground, as a milestone. For a good ten minutes, I had to tamp down the black, worm-eaten earth against the cutting, while "Mother" sat there on a rough rock. Suddenly, a white rabbit appeared, making us jump. After that, we went back on our walk for several hours with Flicka, as if nothing had happened.

At the risk of repeating myself, the black canvas purse was found by the police. Otherwise, I would have dug it up myself. The truth is that only two of us knew where the gold was. So yes, it's safe. It was my mother who told the investigators where to dig. No doubt she cooperated with them on the advice of her lawyer, thinking she would get a reduced sentence in return. In return, they sentenced her to life with a twenty-eight year security sentence, which may be the same as a death sentence, given her advanced age. They got her good…

Ah, an idea comes to me… Knowing Mich-Mich, I know too well that he would never have taken the reckless risk of losing everything by entrusting my mother with the heavy task of protecting the entire loot. He knew too well that the "lobotomized chicken" - as he called her - was not smart enough to ensure her full protection, especially because of her lack of duplicity. It is therefore not excluded that Michel buried another part of the treasure somewhere else. At this point, I would not be surprised. That's all I can tell you, without any more lies.

19.
GOOD RESOLUTIONS

> "Men make their own history,
> but they do not make it arbitrarily, under conditions
> chosen by them, but under conditions
> directly given, and inherited from the past."
> Karl Marx

January 1, 2016, in Paris

On this first day of the year, the little prince of Sautou, who had previously forbidden himself any outburst, made a resolution for the new year. The sweetness of love, and the charms of family commitment... Selim agreed to speak to his sister Anne in person. What a surprise it was for me, at daybreak, to receive the soundtrack of his phone call, made in the Paris region.

Selim. - Hello? .... B... Hello, how are you?
Anne. - Yes, I'm fine, uh... And you?

Selim. - Am I okay? Yes, I'm fine, well... I'm calling you because I want to wish you all the best for this new year that is coming. I'm... I wish you all the best.

Anne. - Well! Happy New Year! Yes. Yes. Yes. Uh, well, that's... that's really nice of you. Thank you very much, uh... I, in turn, wish you and your family all the best. How are you doing? I'm listening to you.

Selim. - It's okay, it's okay... I'm sorry it took me so long to call you. You wrote to me in November 2014, and I'm only calling you in January 2016. It's been cottony. It took me some courage.

Anne. - But, I... I'm sorry, uh... I didn't recognize your voice.

Selim. - It's... it's normal. It's been more than ten years now that...

Anne. - Hey! Who is this? Tell me your name!

Selim. - What is it?

Anne. - Please tell me who you are.

Selim. - This is me, this is Selim.

anne. - How do you do that!

Selim. - I am Selim, your little brother.

Anne. - Oh, no! Selim! That's not true... Oh, the shock! Well... Welcome! It's so good to hear from you. Oh! Really, I wasn't expecting that, no I... It's nice to hear from you. But, where are you? What are you doing?

Selim. - I am at a friend's house, in Nice.

Anne. - So you did receive my mail with my cell phone number?

Selim. - Yes, but... Let's say it took me a while to decide to call you. It wasn't easy at all. I had a lot of trouble.

Anne. - I know, but I had to, and I'm glad. Selim, we absolutely must meet. We must! We must meet, and it will be a pleasure. I would like to welcome you to my home and see what you are like. Besides, I have children to introduce to you. I'd like you to meet my whole family! I think we have a lot to talk about. By the way, Uncle Andre was telling me recently that after what happened where you lived with your parents in Belgium, in Sart-Custinne... Well, before everything was ransacked by the police, he managed to recover some of your belongings. He keeps them preciously in the attic, for you. They are things that are meant for you. Memories. When you feel ready to get them back, you should approach him.

Selim. - That's very nice of him, thank you, but... but, you tell him that I don't need such "memories". For me, it's over. I've left all that behind. I want to draw a definitive line on that time, even if it means pretending to have a goldfish memory. No need to stir up the past.

Anne. - I see. You, unlike us, have had no one else to turn to except those two parents that everyone knows. We know who they are and... Oh, Selim, I thought of you so much!

Selim. - And I'm here too. At first, it was hard not to hear from all of you. No one in sight. Not a thing. Not a single phone call. I was all alone there... It was hard.

Anne. - Yes, I can see that.

Selim. - After, inevitably, in the long run, you get used to it.

Anne. - Yes, you get used to it! You make do with what you have, but well... It's good to hear you, if you only knew... Oh! I'm surprised... I didn't expect it. I didn't even recognize your voice. Of course, you are a man now. I knew you when you were still a child. It's a nice surprise! I'm glad you did! I'm so glad! So for you, all that is really ancient history? You don't want to hold on to any memories? For me, I'm completely oblivious to what happened. This story is not mine.

Selim. - Anne, I don't care about all this junk. All that André could recover... Tsss! It's all false memories. I was fourteen, and everything I believed in was a lie. Burn them, or give them away.

Anne. - I understand you, Selim. You know, I wish I had heard from you sooner. Believe me, I called your last known address many times... I think it was a shelter. They told me that you had left and then they refused to give me your new address. I gave them mine, making them promise to forward it to you, but...

Selim. - I didn't know anything about it. On the other hand, I think I know that André had my brother's address, in Vallauris. Anyway! I've been looking for you for a long time on social networks.

Anne. - Ah, I hate the Internet, considering everything that has happened. You know the saying: to live happily, let's live hidden. Last year, you know, I even found a portrait of you in the press. I recognized you right away! It could only be you! You are handsome. In fact, I printed this picture and kept it with me. I allowed myself!

Selim. - You have done well.

Anne. - And otherwise, is everything okay? The house? Friends? Girls? Working?

Selim. - I provide security in a DIY store, but also in a hotel. All this, while doing some extra work on the side, from time to time. As a result, I have two open-ended contracts. I don't have time to get bored.

Anne. - But financially, are you doing well?

Selim. - There are ups and downs, but overall, I have no complaints. The most important thing is health, isn't it?

Anne. - It's very accurate, and you give the impression of looking good. You also have a nice voice. It's really nice to hear! Say, I could see myself stopping by your place in July. What do you think?

Selim. - I say you are welcome here!

Anne. - I'll do that! On your side, if you decide one day to spend a few days in the Paris area, don't hesitate to let me know. It would be nice to take advantage of it, one way or another. And by the way, do you ever come to Paris?

Selim. - Oh, no, you don't! And I don't like it either. The last time was three years ago, as part of a compulsory training, and I must say that it was not a real pleasure...

Anne. - Don't you like it, Paris?

Selim. - No, frankly, not at all, but don't worry. For you, Anne, I will come! You must know that I am only short of time. The vacations, for me, will not fall soon.

Anne. - It's a deal! So I'm going to plan my next vacation in Nice right now.

Selim. - Perfect.

Anne. - Brother, I have a thirteen year old daughter that I would like you to meet. She was born in December 2002.

Selim. - She is thirteen years old, really? Oh! the slap! I haven't seen you for fourteen years, can you imagine?

Anne. - I remember the last time as if it were yesterday. I had come to see you in Sart-Custinne, when I was pregnant. Later, Michel came to see the baby at the maternity ward, but he was alone. Immediately afterwards, in fact, uh... it... it happened... Ah! and then, time passes. You know, I also have a son who is going to be ten years old. Hey, yes! What do you want me to say? It took you a long time to call me! Oh, my, my... I'm so happy about this! My Selim!

Selim. - Sister, I forgot to tell you something. It is not thanks to me that we are talking now, but thanks to a... journalist!

Anne. - Look, when I got your letter in October 2014, I thought, Well, well...this is weird. It doesn't sound like he's the one talking. He seems to have been pushed into it. I remember reading this interview with you in *VSD*. And then, I thought that this same journalist was perhaps trying to find out about me through you. Selim, I tell you, I prefer discretion to all things. I will not be seen in the media. I only spoke once with a journalist from Le *Figaro*. Let's just say that she seemed more sane than the others. Apart from that, I feel like a stranger to this whole story. I never understood. It was difficult for me. When the affair broke, I was living in Clairefontaine-en-Yvelines. I was the only one who stayed here. It was hard. I was renting my grandmother's house from my own mother. For a month, French and Belgian journalists kept harassing me. It was terrible! They stood there, under the porch, all the time. And if I made the mistake of stepping outside, paparazzi would chase me on motorcycles. It was pure madness! I couldn't leave my garden without being photographed without my knowledge. I had to hide all the time!

Selim. - That journalist I was telling you about, Olivier... Together, we wrote to our father, who included the idea of reuniting us among his follies. Yes, it was Michel who was so keen for me to hear from you, invoking, and I quote, a "family synergy". It was even he who gave me your address. To be honest, I wasn't very excited about writing to you, since nobody had ever heard from me, well...

Anne. - Selim, I understand.

Selim. - And then, one day, this journalist said to me: "Now we are going to write to your sister. So we wrote this letter, and here it is! I have to say that when I received your reply one morning in November 2014, it made me... Well, I have to tell you that it made my heart warm, like never before!

Anne. - You are not alone anymore, Selim. It's over! Your call fills me with joy, if you only knew! I was desperate to hear from you one day, my brother. Ah, if you only knew how happy I am!

Selim. - It took me a while, and I apologize. I was so apprehensive about this call... More than ten years have passed, and I was afraid to interfere in your new life for fear of spoiling everything. Yes! I was afraid of ruining your happiness.

Anne. - Let's see, you are welcome! Ah! Selim! When you were still a child, you used to play tricks on me and my late sister, Marie-Hélène. Ah! Marie-Hélène! You had fun hiding her wallet, or my hat. Ha! Ha! Ha! I assure you! You were always ready to play tricks. Ah! you were so cute... With my sister, when we came to see you at home, we always wondered what joke you were going to invent this time...

Selim: I reassure you. I haven't changed in that respect!

Anne. - Oh, my Selim, before I hang up, there's something I need to talk to you about. You know, Uncle Andre... Selim, you have to understand that he and his wife did not expect this situation that your mother and our father put us in. You must know that Uncle Andre did a lot to help your family. It was even his wife who taught you to read, do you remember that?

Selim. - Yes, yes, I remember it very well!

Anne. - I think it would be a good idea for you to take your courage in both hands and contact Uncle André. You

19. Good resolutions

can't imagine how much it would please him, who has always been so "family", you know...

Selim. - This is indeed the image I kept of him.

Anne. - When I received your letter, he was the first to know. Since that day, he calls me every two or three days to find out if you've answered me or not. He wants to know how you are, where you are... You know, Uncle André is getting old, and he has just turned eighty-six, which is not nothing. It would be a shame if he... Well, I mean... Well, do as you feel, brother. The choice is yours.

Selim. - It's okay, Anne. I'll get in touch with the uncle.

Anne. - Thank you, Selim. He'll be relieved to hear you're okay. He wants to give you your things back, in person.

A Funny Little Voice, *incidental intervention* - Who's on the phone, Mom? Is it Dad?

Anne. - Uh, no... No, it's not dad, honey. It's uh... It's Selim, my brother - or should I say - your uncle. It's uncle Selim!

The little boy. - Uncle Selim?

***

If only you had heard the muffled sobs crackling on both sides of the phone... It was a moment of pure magic. These two succeeded in drawing a tear from my eyes, my mind in celebration, to the point of dancing alone - I confess - a bourrée auvergnate, to the rhythm of a triple hurrah. Ah! what a joy for me to learn this... The sky is not so inflexible. You did the right thing, and I am proud of you. I take my hat off to you, and my wig with it!

At the same time, Michel Fourniret was not insensitive to our last letter. He is now convinced that his son is unwaveringly loyal to him.

Michel Fourniret, *to Selim* - Much more courteous. Bring it on, civilian, is the tone of your last letter. Much more pleasant to read than to have to savor, by letter, flights of hostility. Even if health problems, such as chronic constipation, insomnia or abuse of effervescent cogitations could have been the cause. Phew!

20.
LA MAISON-DIEU

> "You will know the truth,
> and the truth will make you free men.
> The Gospel according to John

January 15, 2016, in Ensisheim

Departure day for the ogre's prison. Selim and I met at the Nice-Côte d'Azur airport for our quest.

Last night, I hardly slept a wink, haunted by the friendly dedication that Mr. Postiche, André Bellaïche, had scribbled on the false title page of his book, which I have kept ever since like a precious relic: "I hope you will get out of *My Life Without Postiche* without breaking and entering." Today, more than ever, these words take on a new meaning, given that I am about to illegally introduce an object into the walls of the Ensisheim power plant...

This object was given to me this morning, after a long week spent worrying about it. In order not to lose a single crumb of the interview with Michel Fourniret, I asked the best contact in the field of espionage in the person of the famous and ingenious paparazzi, Jean-Claude Elfassi. He had the wonderful idea of advising me to buy a spy camera, hidden inside a thumb-thin USB key, whose lens is barely bigger than a fish eye. Often considered evil, I have never received anything but excellent advice from him. He is a careful man, very careful. So when I asked him to teach me the best way to get through the carefully guarded security gates, this is what he told me: "Hide your camera as close to a jeans button as possible. Trust me, the guards won't even notice..."

Between you and me, it shouldn't be that difficult to get a simple USB key into a prison, considering the drugs that pass through there every day... I try to reassure myself by diverting my thoughts, because it has been made clear to me that the crime of smuggling objects into a prison is severely repressed by the law, which everyone is supposed to know. One year in prison, at the very least. Let us consider, please, the extension of the state of emergency decreed after the attacks of November 13. Surveillance has since been reinforced, given the tension in the country. Admittedly, this comes at a rather bad time, but hey...

"So, let me get this straight, fatty! you got a pass with the management's consent. First of all, don't bring the whole mess with you right away. It's better to test the waters on the first date. Take advantage of this to find the ideal hideout. In any case, don't hide your stuff under your armpits. The guards will definitely ask you to raise your arms. Hey, you know what... I know! Just shove your USB stick up your ass like it's a pot stick. That's how it works, fatty!"

Standing in the doorway of a large shopping mall, I spot a familiar, lone figure in the airport fast food joint. This dear prince of Sautou sits on a plastic throne, dressed in a hunting jacket with a brown leather strap sewn on his shoulders. He gulps down a hamburger, without even chewing it.

Here you are, you little joker...," I said, going towards his cluttered table.

- Not had time to eat t'à l'heure!" he growls, between two mouthfuls of crocodile.

Then we both run to the boarding gate of our flight to Basel-Mulhouse airport. At the sector assigned to the Swiss services, Selim passes through without a hitch. As for me - and I was a little suspicious because of my registration in the T.A.J. - a Smurf wearing a finely worked kepi is going to hold my leg, causing a pile-up in the queue. "Passport! Passport!" Tucked behind his gatehouse, the guard with sad mustaches, topped with heavy eyelids, frowns, no doubt reading the information that spouts from his computer screen.

Halt there!" he throws, with morgue. Where are you going?

- Um... In Mu... In Mulhouse, sir," I stammered.

I finally leave the control zone, without a blow.

***

Selim, sitting on my right on the window side, keeps his usual attitude of a beaten dog. I look at him attentively in a contemplative silence, while he mocks a stewardess, busy explaining to a young man how to unlock the emergency exit next to his seat.

I don't know why we have come to talk about sex in front of such a large audience, but Selim starts to extol the virtues of the oldest profession in the world again, in such a way that I suddenly find it painful to be in his company. I signal him to be quiet. Am I to understand that you continue to lead a dissolute life, to the rhythm of long hours of thankless work, of insomnia bounces, and of devastating follies? Lacking the most elementary reserve, he then makes, in majesty, a panegyric of a woman named Lola. About twenty, no more. According to the report, she is a young Romanian woman with a delicate face, with whom he had fallen in love the evening before. Let us note that before picking her enormous breasts that the wind made beat, he had to unload, by handfuls, of a rainbow of hard-earned banknotes. Three hundred euros in small bills.

Lola is in his eyes a noble and respectable lady. Let's not be afraid of the words. A man of perfect education - despite his DNA -, the cheerful Selim, with his most graceful air, slowly lays his protruding chin in his palm, and lets out a long, deep sigh.

I can't wait to see her again," he said, "if only to chat a little and give her some nice kisses...

- Don't say any more, I beg you! I say, yawning. Just why didn't you try your luck on the dating site I told you about? What do you have to lose? You might be surprised, you know. Go ahead, try your luck!

- No.

- And why not?

- The answer is quite simple, answers Selim, blushing.

-Oh yeah? You know... you're not any uglier than anyone else."

And, with a bit of melancholy, Selim, slumped on his seat, his complexion frazzled, shakes his head like a shell, shrugging his shoulders a bit, and says to me gravely:

"But no! No way! I leave that to the real handsome, which I am not," he says, as if it were obvious, and adds: "I do not feel capable, that's all.

Selim is at the very least a polite, good-looking boy. He is honest, hardworking, sober, thoughtful, and moreover very resourceful. What moves me so strongly, above all, is his ability to survive in all circumstances, when some people too easily opt for death at the slightest difficulty.

Twenty minutes later, I am pulled out of my sleep by a series of turbulences. The plane starts its descent.

By the way," I said casually. I still can't believe that the father of your colleague Thomas could also be there.

- Well! Last week," Selim continues, "Thomas received a call from him. You'll never guess... He confided that he had often come across a man named Mich-Mich in the prison yard.

- What are you saying! Are you kidding?" I replied, all confused.

Selim then nods glumly. "Once he was his chess partner. He said that the ogre usually broods over all sorts of evils, alone in a corner. He doesn't talk to anyone, and no one talks to him. Finally, he would have disappeared from circulation for almost a year. Strange, isn't it? On the contrary, none of this is surprising. Michel Fourniret is rumored to be suffering from Parkinson's disease. Do we ever know? If he is telling the truth, it could be that his health has deteriorated to the point of requiring his bed rest. If so, we will soon find out. It's getting cold... " Land in sight!" says Selim.

***

The night is dark. After a short passage to the baggage carousel in the Basel-Mulhouse-Freiburg airport, we are plunged into confusion, and as soon as we pass the porch, we are greeted by a hailstorm. Most of the people around us speak German. What planet have we fallen on?

Quickly we manage to get out and find a cab. I knock then a window. On board, a nice grey girl with a boyish haircut. She greets us with an appreciable cordiality, in a French mixed with an improbable accent. "Ensisheim, siouplé! Without warning, the one who answers to the name of Mam'zelle Archon launches into an adventurous course of history, for our biggest pleasure.

Oh, Ensisheim!...," she says, in a honeyed voice. On November 7, 1492, a meteorite of 135 kilos came crashing down on Ensisheim. That's a bit of a mouthful, isn't it?

In passing, Archon informs us that the name of our destination is pronounced very exactly [Haine-si-saïm][21] . The prince of Sautou has a smile. The old lady continues: It's right there, next door, at equal distance from Colmar and Mulhouse, right in the middle," the lady details, drawing a triangle with her fingers half-covered with mittens, "a little over half an hour from here, at the gates of the vineyard. It will cost you 50 euros, not a penny more. Come on! Don't just stand there... The car of these gentlemen is advanced. Get in, but only on condition that I get paid in advance! Selim spontaneously opens the door for me, and invites me to slip into the back seat of the cab which, under my weight, starts to rock...

"Say, Mrs. Archon, this is a curious thing, all the same. Where are we?

- You are here in the so-called Three Border Area," says Archon, in a surprisingly pleasant voice. You may not

---

21. [ẽnsisajm]

know it, but Alsace is part of the French-German-Swiss trinational area of the Upper Rhine, called Oberrhein, and here we are precisely at the intersection of the three borders between the cantons of Basel, Baden and Alsace. This is so interesting that I am taking notes on my notebook, so to speak, lest this valuable information be lost forever. Please, may the night be long... Sleep... Sleep...

Some twenty minutes later, by a towpath surrounded by the twists and turns of the Ill river and the Neuf-Brisach canal, here we are in the basement of the hotel called the Domaine du Moulin. The skies, nauseous and conspicious, vomit a thick drizzle on us. Suddenly, under a smoky lamp, the shining lights of the silent Selim reappear. Judging by his funnel-shaped mouth, this oasis of refinement and opulence seems to delight him. With its half-timbered façade, ornate windows and corner oriel, the Domaine du Moulin *was* built in the purest Rhineland architectural style. It has 65 rooms, and features a Spa with swimming pool, sauna, hammam, gym, and outdoor Jacuzzi. "Ah!" said the Prince of Sautou, stunned, seeing in the distance, his nose pressed against the glass, the contours of this establishment surrounded by fine garlands of light. "It is sumptuous! Of my writing gladiolée, in legs of fly, I trace, of the index finger, this sentence decorated with arabesques on a window fogged of the cab: " Who, Anne? "

According to the plan, the Domaine du Moulin borders the rue de la Première Armée française, which is set at right angles to the southern facade of the prison, where the "ogre of the Ardennes" is held. Here is the central prison of Ensisheim, as it was built more than two hundred years ago, under the orders of Emperor Napoleon himself. See for yourself! The prison and the hotel face each other.

Meanwhile, Fourniret's son and I entered the hotel through a revolving door, leading to a vast, high room with a wood-panelled ceiling, where a large chandelier was blazing. We get the keys of our room at the reception, a counter with rounded angles behind which stands a lady in a brown suit, wearing a cloche hat, that Selim immediately tries to flirt with by blabbering an orgy of nonsense. I swear, this idiot cuts him a flap, the foam foaming at the edge of the lips. "The number of your room is 101," she says in an imperious tone, making him understand that he'd better pack up his little cavorting act. "It's on the second floor. I hope you have a pleasant stay in Ensisheim."

Before that, taking advantage of a favorable draft to my vile designs, I sneak to the bar of the hotel, where I am served a superb glass of amber syrup. Just a tear, a hint of a bottle already very much started. Soothing my thirst like an old horse, the noggin plunged in the bottom of a bowl, Selim growls:

"Come on, let's get out of here! But hurry up! I'm hungry!

- If we have to die tomorrow, let it be after having emptied one last bottle of rum!

- It's out of the question that all my euros go into the tord-boyaux. I'm already struggling enough to pay my rent, and to repay the loan of the motorcycle", laments this damned john, visibly stubborn, by pulling the sleeve of my red sweater.

Then he adds:

"Soiffard, go!

- That's it! You poor thing! Console yourself!" I shouted, hilarious. Go tell that to your Lola... that you are penniless... just to see what she says... Huh? Pff!"

***

Thrown in the cosmic night, the stomach in the heels, the prince of Sautou and I beat the macadam, with hurried steps, in the main street of the village, shaving the walls of the prison, where shreds of cloth dance at the points of the barbed wires! This is how the image of an escaped prisoner tortured in screaming agony imposes itself on my imagination, his entrails flayed on a wire covered with blackened blood.

Given the cold weather here, we'd better go and take refuge in some gargote, and in a hurry. We decide to go to La Calèche, a last-rate tavern, which opens its doors only during the prison's working hours, i.e. twice a week. The place isn't very reputable, but it's not as if we had a lot of choice. In the town, there is no competition. Ensisheim seems to be full of shut-ins...

As soon as we passed the door of the estaminet, we were welcomed by the mistress of the house, a woman with a pointed nose and heavy earrings, whom we nicknamed Polenta, as her yellow hair reminded me of the famous cornmeal cake. Let's say it, this lady, well over thirty, is dressed like a faggot: in pumps, and pink silk stockings.

"Have these gentlemen chosen?"

- A bottle of rum," I said, placing my jacket on the back of the empty chair opposite, "and three glasses of equal measure! Then I turned to Selim: "Let's drink the same amount! That will put us back on our feet..."

I note in passing that the hostel in which we are established is located only 9 meters as the crow flies from the penitentiary, where some of the worst crazies in the universe - including Francis Heaulme, Guy Georges, and so on - are just there, fidgeting, spinning in circles in their cell, dreaming of only one thing: to regain their freedom to satisfy their bloodthirsty voracity ... I shiver! There, now, I raise my glass, full to the brim:

"May we, tomorrow morning, get enough information from the ogre to get our hands on the Posthumous treasure. Let's go! Let's drink to the memory of old Myszka! Cheers!

- Happiness for the beggars[22] ! recites in his turn Selim, by making his ball tinkle against mine. On the other hand, there is a very real risk that Mich-Mich refuses to leave his thebaid...

- Well, if that's going to happen, at least we'll leave with the feeling that we've gone all the way. We had to do it. It would have been so foolish not to try anything... To win without peril... Anyway, you know the saying...

- Besides," Selim continues, "it would probably be wise to establish an attack strategy for tomorrow morning. If there's anything left of this treasure, I want to know about it, as much as you do. I may have known Mich-Mich all my life," he warned, "but I won't really get to know him until tomorrow morning. For the first time in my life, I will see him as he is, in his purest form. A pedophile murderer. When we were living under the same roof, Michel Fourniret was undercover. But he knows that I now know the whole truth about his actions. He can no longer hide. There is no way out. I would like to understand why... to move on...

- How can you say that! Never, during all these years spent at his side, did he confide in you that he had been in prison for a dozen sexual assaults on minors[23]?

____

22. Reference to the song *Tant qu'il y aura des étoiles*, song of Tino Rossi.
23. On June 26, 1987, Michel Fourniret was sentenced by the Assize Court of Essonne to five years in prison with three years probation.

Negative. I learned all this on television, like everyone else. In front of me, this bastard was playing a role. He was lying all the time. He was never honest. In fact, I don't know him. He is a stranger. I'm still curious to see his face when he sees us come in tomorrow morning..."

Ah! I conceive, oh prince of Sautou, what your sorrow must be. If I don't tell you so as not to inconvenience you, I am moved. You have guts, uncle. Know that I admire you ardently for your bravery, you, the bait. No matter how much you repeat to anyone who will listen that you owe your life only to your cowardice, I don't believe it. Your very presence in Alsace explicitly demonstrates this. You don't back down in front of the ogre. Let's go! Courage then, my friend. Gird up your loins. We have never been so close to the goal. I'm right here. I'm watching your back. Silently, I pray now that your faith will not fail tomorrow, when you face the mighty boss at the end of the level. By my watch, it is full midnight, the time of Hamlet's ghost on the walls of Elsinore. With this vision strongly imprinted in my mind, little by little, I fade away in my dreams, emptied of all substance, exhausted with fatigue. The day will come.

***

The cock crows twice. It is at the point of dawn, around 7 o'clock, that I regain my spirits scattered to the four corners of my nightmares, like a quartered prisoner. Get up. This is a historic day. As the sun rises to open the day's quarry, my head buzzes so loudly that I think I hear an out-of-tune piano playing. "Come on, get up, lazybones!"

I see an ashen glow emerge from his soot-ringed eyes. And while he slowly gets up from his hatch, stiff as an "L",

I begin to dress, while thinking: I can't wait for this sordid event, in which I am now an actor, to end with a strong chapter, so that I can get out of Michel Fourniret's brain in which I have been stuck for too long...

In less than an hour, I will meet the "ogre of the Ardennes". "Good!" I said to Selim, picking up a brioche with pearl sugar on a slice of bread that had all sorts of sweets on it. "Here we are at work. We're going to do some tests. Listen carefully. At no time must your father suspect that I am a journalist. That's the rule.

- How! But which instruction?" he is astonished, the ear to the listening, while dodging, by agile jumps, my innumerable postillions. "No, I don't agree! I do not know this instruction.

- No, really! You didn't fall on your head, did you? If he knew, it would cause an unprecedented diplomatic crisis. Make sure, Selim, that you make him spit out the location of the remains of the treasure? Don't forget to ask him if he has received the real/false picture of Esau. Did the ogre attend the trial of the late Christian Ranucci in 1976 or not? Between them, the resemblance is total. It is imperative that we solve the mystery surrounding their apparent perfect twinship. Remember, Selim, the great judicial errors! Patrick Dils... Nothing, however, allows us to deny the hypothesis of a relationship between the two. Let's get to the bottom of the Esau theory, shall we? I would even say: let's get to the bottom of the Michel Fourniret theory!

Having said these words, I asked him about the disappearance of Estelle Mouzin, and this is what he told me.

"Selim, did you knowingly consent to serve as an alibi for the ogre, regarding his disappearance?

- What the fuck! What are you talking about?" says Selim, upset, dropping his buttered toast into his coffee.

-You didn't know?

- What the hell am I doing here? What is this story again?

- To make a long story short, Estelle Mouzin disappeared on January 9, 2003, in Guermantes, Seine-et-Marne. Among the evidence against Michel, there is a photograph of the girl that was found on the hard drive of his laptop, but also the recording of television newscasts that speak of her. In the weeks leading up to the abduction, a classmate of Estelle's was allegedly approached after school by a gray-haired man in his 40s, if not older. He insisted on giving her a ride in a white van. Miraculously, she firmly refused. In any case, thanks to the sincere description she was able to give to the police, a black and white sketch of the suspect was established, more or less resembling Michou, who knows the region well having resided there for a time, at a friend's house, after his release from prison in 1987. Didn't you know that?

- Hell no, again! How is he on this sketch?"

As real pictures speak better than bad journalists, I pull out of my pocket a photograph showing a European type individual, relatively dark skin, full eyebrows, and oval glasses. Even more astonishing, it is specified in the description that he would be "likely to have a short beard of several days". Could it be? Is that you, Esau?

"Surely," says Selim, tilting his head, "the look, and the facial expression are familiar to me, but nothing more," he continues, while drinking milk directly from the carton.

- On May 21, 2010, the lawyer for the family of Estelle Mouzin asked the courts to examine three seals from the ogre's file. Two pieces were of particular interest to the lawyer: pieces of white shoelaces and black gloves that could belong to the young girl. Michel would then have defended himself by presenting an alibi: he was in Belgium the day of Estelle's disappearance. Thus, the investigators dismissed the case.

- What does this have to do with me?

- In addition to the fact that your mother lied when she assured the authorities that your father was present in Sart-Custinne at the time of Estelle Mouzin's disappearance, I noted a disturbing element. To consolidate his alibi, Michel said that he had spent the evening on the phone with his son from 8 p.m. onwards from his Belgian home, 400 kilometers from Guermantes, while Estelle disappeared around 6 p.m. on her way home from school".

Selim smiles when he hears this, then laughs out loud:

"What is this story?

- But perhaps he was referring to his other sons?"

Then, gravely:

"Let's not kid ourselves! Nicolas died in 1996. As for Jean-Christophe, I don't know a damn thing about it. As far as I'm concerned, I don't remember having a personal line in 2003. It's simple. I didn't make or receive any phone calls except from the home landline. Come on! I was 15 years old... In those days, cell phone use was not common. What's more, he never called me in his life to check up on me, let alone in the middle of the night. I've never had a cop talk to me about this. It's ridiculous!"

***

Arrived at the height of the prison, Selim hurries in front of two armoured doors. Under a tricolor flag flapping in the four winds, a crowd without number of wrapped up visitors come from everywhere, and brought by buses specially chartered. Let us position ourselves behind them, along these metal posts arranged at regular intervals. As I pull my cap down, as soon as I enter, my eye is drawn to a petrifying figure trying to scale the prison's façade. A sculpture with the figure of an old grunt, choked by two vile boas snakes. His almond-shaped eyes are crinkled under the effect of torture.

The central house of Ensisheim has had various destinations over the centuries. Built in 1452 as a civil hospital, this building became a school in 1551 when the hospital was moved to rue de la Bonbonnière. In 1570, the former royal school was transformed into the Saint-Erhard seminary by the priest Rasser, a preacher of the Counter-Reformation. Religion and literature were taught there. After his death in 1594, it was replaced by a Jesuit college based on specific teachings, known in Ensisheim through the work of Johann Jacob Balde. This professor of rhetoric, preacher at the court of Munich, poet, philosopher, visionary and successor of the humanists did not live in Ensisheim but was born there in 1604. In 1773, the college was transformed into a depository for beggars and convicts from the correctional courts of Alsace. It received old men and women, orphans, beggars, vagabonds, lunatics, idiots and girls of ill repute. In 1795, the begging depot was replaced by a military hospital and a depot for suspects. In 1811, by imperial decree, the establishment was converted into a central house of force and correction. After the closure of the colonial prisons in 1938, those sentenced to forced labor were sent here to serve their sentences.

***

"Clack!" A small window in the prison's porte cochere opens. A blue cap is seen in a bright quadrangular opening. A jailer arrives, his weapon in his arm, making his boots squeak on the square. He shouts, his nose riveted to a sheaf of paperwork: "Fourniret family!" Around us, the prosaic crowd is making awful clamors. And, in this confused rumour, I distinguish this remark repeated of a high and sonorous voice: "Hey! Fourniret, the pedophile?" Another replies, stretching his face toward us, "Do you think those are his little ones?" And again, the sentry: "Fourniret family! Selim, delivered without precautions to the public opprobrium, suddenly pulls his neck into his shoulders wrapped in a scarf, as if he had just been stabbed to the flesh with a dagger.

"How strange," he says, as curled up as an old parchment can be, "I hadn't been called that for ten years. With that, he begins his way of the cross. As we move forward under the booing, the other visitors stand out in our path, like a swarm of frightened pigeons. So I say to him gravely in a whisper, amidst the jeers: "Never mind the chatter. Just act like we're in a movie, and we'll be fine."

Between you and me, it was not very clever of the deer to call us in this way, especially since the name of the Beast does not appear on any official document, having been disowned for a long time, as if Selim was orphaned of father and mother. This is a fact. As of October 2, 2007, no petition has been registered with the Secretariat of the Contentious Division of the Council of State in opposition to the decree of April 26, 2007, published in the Official Journal of the French Republic on April 29, 2007, which authorized Fourniret Selim, Gwenhaël, Jean-Pierre, to change his surname, the purpose being to combat the prejudices that oppose his development.

Silence is achieved. In the purgatory shaded by a curtain of bars, a guard on duty stands near the wall. Behind a plexiglass window, a fat phlegmatic lady, submits us to an identity check, to which I stick first, without batting an eyelid. "Here are my identity papers. Then comes Selim's turn, and the first squeak sounds.

"You are not on the list," thunders the lady, phlegmatically, turning the pages of the register. "I will be obliged to keep you here while waiting for instructions". I interpose by saying in a contentious tone:

"But finally, madam! This is ridiculous! There must be a mistake!

- I am sorry, she said, it is impossible for me to let him continue on his way...

- Listen to me. He is Michel Fourniret's son, not me! I'm just his companion... This is a big mistake! I'm not going alone! This is unheard of!"

In front of this protocol absurdity, I put the forehead in my hands, and remain thus the time that she realizes her error. All reverence kept, she orders us to leave the metals at the door of the temple, by indicating to us transparent racks, under a row of umbrellas. Selim undresses then his coat, that he rolls in ball. By disengaging me, it returns to me by flashes the words of the wise Elfassi: to dissimulate the camera "near a zipper, or a button", the goal being to escape the vigilance of the guards, by sowing confusion in their spirit. While my companion takes off his shoes, I rummage in my bag, the eye which curls, in corner, and withdraw the USB key, which I slip stealthily in the pocket gusset of my pants to the over-stitched seams, with a few centimeters of a metal disc covered with a layer of nickel. We then put our shoes on the conveyor belt. On his side, Selim passes under the gantry, and lands on the other side without a hitch. The guard signals to me to move forward in turn. My breath is taken away. I risk everything. I stop for a moment, I wait, and then I cross the finish line, my face flushed... A bell rings clearly. "Hey, wait a minute! He's got a penknife in his pants pocket!" the other owl cries out from behind his unwashed window, eyes glued to the dials on his console. In a flash, the owl clutches my arm, shaking me disapprovingly:

"Hey! Stop there! What's in that pocket? Sir, do you have a dagger? One last time," the man said impatiently, "do you have a knife or something? I advise you not to make a fool of me! And faster than that!

- Me? Oh!" I protested, ironically, in the manner of Louis de Funès, while pretending to search my pockets to better shuffle my cards. Absolutely not! It's a very funny mistake. See! Where would it be, this knife? In the other pocket, no doubt... Damn! Not in this one either... ! It's probably the button of my jeans which is at the origin of this...

- Well, the rookie interrupts me, it's really taking the piss out of the world! Well, we'll see about that!"

The situation turns to our disadvantage. Selim's arms fall off. How will I get out of this one? Caught in a vice, with a bayonet in my back, I don't know how to make up for it. Trying the devil at a time when the anti-terrorist alert level is at its peak, I really had to be crazy! How could I have believed, for a single moment, that I would manage to fool a millimeter wave body scanner, without taking the precaution of greasing the paw of the security guard with fifty biftons? Suddenly, the big vein that runs vertically down the middle of my forehead swells up prodigiously, suggesting an imminent explosion.

"Guilty, me? You dare to accuse me? Well! this knife..." I said, pulling the object of the crime from my pocket, looking falsely indignant. Here it is! I found it! See thus! See, before you stick your bayonet in my thighs. The parcel bomb is nothing more than a simple USB key, which I failed to dispose of. You had the flair. Indeed, I made an oversight. I'm sorry about that!

- It's okay, let him pass," said a voice behind me.

Excusing my alleged blunder, the guard felt me up and finally authorized me to enter the visiting rooms. Not totally fooled, he orders me to deposit the blunt object with the rest of my belongings. I don't need to submit to the diktat of the image anyway, at least as long as my memory remains intact... It's a good thing I chose this model of camera in the form of a computer data storage tool! I dare not imagine what would have happened if they had guessed my real intention. Stripped of my personal objects, I can finally dash into a corridor lit by an oblique window, at the end of which Selim is waiting for me. Standing, feet in square, we are asked to wait between walls tinted in green.

What was that flash drive doing in your pocket?" he says in my ear in a startled whisper. It was a camera, wasn't it? But why didn't you tell me? Don't you know the risks involved?

- Shh! Listen to this instead, Uncle... those sounds... like artillery discharges... Can you hear them, too?"

After ten minutes, the landing door of the dungeon swings on its hinges in a powerful hum. After having climbed a revolving staircase composed of 33 steps separated by a rest, and leading straight to Golgotha, we pass no less than three security locks, empty of any presence, and whose only ornaments are iron-lined blast doors, bulletproof glass windows, and video surveillance cameras. Another stopover! We will stay there for a good ten minutes. Funny thing, the walls are scratched, and the doors are studded with traces of blows, as if other visitors, before us, had literally lost all patience.

The last secured passage has just been unlocked... Shouts of voices rise, some low, others high. Just before taking my momentum, I lapped up a thin stream of lukewarm water from the tap.

Selim as well as myself are introduced by three big knocks. In a few martial strides, we enter the eye of the storm, a dilapidated room with a high ceiling, a glass door, violently lit with neon, with two long rows of glass booths in its middle. Another detail, the wall of the northern facade is pierced with some barricaded windows with opaque glass. Without disassembling, Selim advances with the step of an automaton in front of a small counter, jostling everything on his way, including an old man slumped, in dirty clothes, surrounded by whistling and undulating railings. There, a new owl, very high perched, the face slightly inclined towards the front, asks in which capacity he comes to announce himself in these places:

"I am Selim, and I have come to visit my father, the so-called "Ogre of the Ardennes".

- What's his name?" the owl asks, his hands clasped in the shape of a roof, from his perch.

- Fourniret Michel, declines Selim, his lip dropping a little. Can I wait for him here?

- But... hey! Your daddy, dear sir... Hey!" she chuckles, in a perspicacious tone, "Bah!" he's there, right there, behind you."

As he says this, Selim twists his moustache and puts his hand on his bushy arches. We realize whose silver beard this is, topped by a ravished face, all set with flat-headed nails for eyes - the ones we just met in front of the coffee machine. A shiver of anguish suddenly seizes me. Then Selim turns to him with a calmness that only stoics have the secret of, and says to him imperiously: "Is that you? I had not recognized you..."

Father and son did not recognize each other, each being struck by the strangeness of the other's appearance. Michel Fourniret constantly makes these exclamations, his mouth wide open and his eyes round. Each of his sentences seems to have for exordium "Oh!"; "Oh! Oh! Oh! Really, Selim? Is it you? Oh, my goodness... Oh, yes, it is you! Here you are! ; Oh! So there! It's my son!" Under the blow of the surprise, he nods of the head, by giving to his mouth a cute shape, then undergoes a numbness, putting himself to vacillate here and there, slow and heavy. His heavy waxy eyelids flutter, clearing two snowy eyebrows that bar his face. "Oh! Oh!" Onomatopoeia abounds, and then the reunion dance opens.

There stands the almighty enemy, firmly planted on his legs, of flesh and bone. He is "Shere Khan", the ogre with golden iron and sparkling blue eyes, the one who constantly speaks in riddles, and heaps ruin upon ruin in such large torrents, throwing tortured children at his feet. The same one who dared to defy, in his time, the gotha of the Parisian underworld, ignoring the threats until raising himself to the rank of squire.

Aware of not being very presentable to Selim, at this very moment, Michel Fourniret starts dusting his grey "V" knit with its eliminated collar. The *same goes* for his mended beige pants, all speckled with white paint splashes, although there is nothing left to show for it. His glasses did not resist the conditions of incarceration either, one of the broken temples being roughly wrapped with a yellowed, dusty adhesive tape. What can we say, too, about his brown woven leather loafers, which, though they have a remnant of splendor, scream bafflement. The contrast between them is striking. One would almost believe to see a rough stone, crumbly on all sides, contrary to Selim - a real little pebble from Nice - who opposes him a hairless face, admirably shaved, as if worked with a chisel.

As for his physical appearance, apart from his hygiene and his pallid complexion, it is undeniable that it has not been altered in the least, as if the blood siphoned from his victims had allowed him to prolong his existence. Behind the scraggly hairs of her shaggy beard, her skin is surprisingly smooth and spotless. Seventy-four years old, and no tonsure, nothing! Three times nothing! So, yes, his hair is silver, but it is abundant, and silky... Think, by way of comparison, of the thirty-year-old goats of my McDonald's and Coca-Cola generation. How many of them already have such a pathetically peeled head? Similarly, Selim, year after year, has seen his hairline recede several centimeters, forming an "M" as in "cursed" to the top of his head, prompting him to regularly shave low, close to the leather. All this becomes logical if we consider that the "ogre of the Ardennes" is not concerned by the hard work. What an injustice towards our poor parents who break their backs, crumpled and soiled by lowly tasks, while the detention of a pedophile is done in a temporality without real flow, only punctuated by meals at fixed hours. What baseness, and what infamy is it not to pamper a pedophile murderer, at the expense of the honest taxpayer.

Another amusing detail - if one can split a pear in a cabin - Michel Fourniret may be one of the most terrifying serial killers in criminal history, but I find him rather short-legged. Indeed, contrary to the image of greatness that he may have projected because of the fear inspired by his infinite cruelty, he is, in my eyes, only half a man. The terrible "ogre of the Ardennes" measures precisely 1,67 meter *and half*, while the prince of Sautou, him, culminates at 1,87 meter.

"At the time when we lived in Belgium, he would confide in me later, Mich-Mich often felt the need to remind anyone who wanted to hear that he was 1.67 meters tall, half a centimeter taller than a politician, whose name escapes me... ". Christian Ranucci was 1.73 meters tall...

I deduce that Selim got his tall height from his mother Monique Olivier, whom the ogre nicknamed his "chickadee", after a very small bird of the order of the passerines. I will learn from Selim's mouth that she is "immense", so much so that she is several heads taller than her "fawn", her "tiger", her "favorite little convict", as she liked to call him.

Another notable fact is that no physical contact was established between Selim and Michel Fourniret. Not the slightest sign of affection. Never a tender gesture. I scrupulously make sure to keep my hands in my pockets, while taking care to avoid any elbowing. I formally refuse to shake hands with a child executioner, guilty of the most detestable crimes.

Then comes the moment to lead us backwards, on order of the jailer, towards a large transparent cube duly covered, under a well of light. This one is flanked by an opaque screen made of sanded glass. This is used as a cover for couples during the rut, provided, of course, that the occasion is appropriate. With small steps, I slip away, bowing like a liveryman, inviting the prince, accompanied by the vile snake, to penetrate first in the box of 3 m2, buried in the silence.

The moment Michel Fourniret walks past me, I am struck by a great calamity, the rapid pulse. But... how is this possible? The serial killer is in possession of a well-sharpened pencil-eraser, clasped in the gutter of a small sketch pad, outlined by spiral arcs, which he holds wedged under his arm. I take note of another, equally terrifying discovery: his fists have not been handcuffed. Stop me if I'm wrong, but in such cases, shouldn't he be bound hand and foot? Instead, Michel Fourniret is free, entirely free here to make us one-eyed, if he wishes...

As soon as I crossed the threshold of the cube, I misjudged my strength. "Clack!" Anxious to leave the door ajar, the trapdoor fell noisily on its hinges under the imperturbable eye of Michel Fourniret, whose attention wanes. What the hell are you doing?" asks the reckless Selim. Is there a problem?" I think for a few seconds. "On the rest of the front, nothing to report", I object, entrenched behind a malicious smile of command, sprinkled with a yellow laugh.

I try to open the damn door again. The truth is, it's locked. We are locked inside a glass box with a notorious serial killer armed with a mechanical pencil to sketch my portrait. I can't believe it, as the turn of events resembles the denouement of a psychological thriller, with the only difference that Michel Fourniret is not a fictional character, like Hannibal Lecter. Here, everything is real. There is no way out. From now on, almost anything can happen, the best or the worst. I fear that Michel Fourniret, if the discussion makes him angry, will let his fury go unchecked.

In the middle of the glass cube, a totem of buttercup chairs is enthroned. Unashamedly, Selim, set up as a leader, takes a step to the right, grabs three of them and suddenly tumbles them forward, until they form an inverted pyramid. At the same time, he indicates to his father where to settle down, throwing: "Sit down! Tassé and grumpy, Michel Fourniret, carries out this order by taking the place which is assigned to him, as it has just been said. Short pause. Silence is established. Once the back leaned against the back of the chair, whose feet seem to have been sawn off, Michel Fourniret, already so small, is swallowed up, until his knobby knees bend at right angles, suddenly giving the impression of being caught by a column of shifting sand, almost at ground level.

I just realized why the ogre seems to have undergone some planing. The prince of Sautou has given him a child's chair. It is there of a completed ridiculousness. What an aesthetic shock, decidedly! The manipulative pervert dressed of oripeaux resembles here a child claiming the breast, the shaggy hair. What a bewildering spectacle! On the *contrary,* Selim and myself seem two judges ready to direct the debates with a mallet, at the aplomb of a promontory.

Michel Fourniret, *motionless* - Oh! Selim? I never thought I'd find you here. Never! I didn't even recognize you. Oh! As far as I can see, little Selim is no more. At twenty-seven, Selim Gwenhael Jean-Pierre? Not really a kid anymore... Oh! Two months ago, you told me you wanted to come here. I tried to dissuade you then. Maybe I was wrong.

Selim, *in a very low voice* - You're wrong, it was a year ago now. Since you never answer clearly in your letters, I came to challenge you to a duel. Face to face. I demand answers. No more beating around the bush!

Michel Fourniret. - Oh! I really didn't expect it to be you.

Selim, *his eyes half closed* - Didn't anyone tell you I was coming?

Michel Fourniret. - A guard appeared out of nowhere, just twenty minutes ago. I, quite stupidly, thought at first that the prosecutor wanted to hear me again in the Estelle Mouzin case. I assure you that I have nothing to do with it. I know what I did and what I didn't do. I am right in my boots, Selim! Anyway, it's not for me to say if I did this or that... To arrest me? The police lacked the evidence! Let them bring me some evidence, and I'll decide! Anyway, that's when the guard explained to me that I had visitors in the visiting room. For me, it could only be a mistake. How could I have guessed? This is the first time I have had visitors...

Selim. - And yet! With mom, we had come to visit you several times at the prison of Dinant. It was just before you were transferred and she was arrested in turn for covering up your schemes. Really, you don't remember that?

Michel Fourniret, *pouting* - No... no... no... Oh, it's you, Selim. I feel like I'm looking at Monique Olivier. No one will be able to say that you have inherited the physical features of your old father. Oh, that! You are the spitting image of your mother. Resemblance of the faces ? It is enough to compare the photo of your face fixed to your identity card, of which I have a copy, and the features of that of your mother, to be justified in exclaiming: such a mother, such a son!

Selim. - And you are the spitting image of your brother.

Michel Fourniret, *taking a more serious tone* - Oh! Selim, as guilty as I am, you must understand that Monique Olivier is very well where she is. Her place is in prison. You know as well as I do that she does not have any kind of qualification, nor education. Your mother lacks independence. On her own, she would have been unable to support herself. She would have put herself in danger. No, really, she would never have survived out there alone... Believe me, Selim! Behind bars, she at least benefits from a competent supervision allowing her to continue to live in all serenity.

Selim, *deaf to her insinuations* - How are you doing?

Michel Fourniret, *puffing out his chest* - Everything is going well! Even if I spend years there, I'll manage to convince you that in prison, well, I've entered nirvana. Oh, nir-va-na!... I am certainly freer here than anywhere else. What can a free citizen boast of? He is only free to work, to pay taxes, to do the shopping, to wash the dishes, to assume - at least badly - the burden of the thousand and one chores of a daily life that repeats itself from one decade to another, 365 days a year. Bastard tax collectors! Constantly on my tail! As far as I was concerned, my status as a free citizen was replaced by the privileged status of a gracious prisoner of the Prison Service. Here, I am housed, heated, fed, whitened, and free to use my time, twenty-four hours a day, seven days a week! And since the State has made me its guest, I can freely devote myself to writing whenever I want. My only task today is - I confess - to put my empty plate in the sink after lunch, and that's about it. In the past, I used to play chess, but I preferred to stop the damage, because the level of my opponents was so low. Otherwise, I read the newspaper twenty minutes every morning, listening to France Culture, or Radio Classique. State of emergency?

O poor France! Marianne clenches her buttocks! Enough talk... The Hexagon! In a state of war! Every day, I enjoy these exceptional privileges, in the most total freedom.

Selim, *annoyed* - I think it's sad that you're happy to be in prison. Besides, prison is not free. Do you realize that it's people like me who work hard to pay for prisoners' incarceration costs? If you are free, it is only because I am your prisoner...

Michel Fourniret, *with emphasis* - I thus dare to believe proverbially that it is necessary to be taken to be learned. Without laces, nor suspenders, rid of everything that ties and holds me back, I learn to live again. I enter into existence!

Selim, *his voice full of weariness* - By the way, it was reported to me that you suffer from an incurable disease... Are you sick, is it true?

Michel Fourniret, *listening* - Is he right? I didn't quite understand. Can you repeat what you said? I've become a bit hard of hearing with age, you know...

Selim, *raising his index finger* - Do you have Parkinson's disease?

Under the effect of this last sentence, the "ogre of the Ardennes" is overcome by a terrible spasm, which makes him fall backwards. What does this mean? Taken of convulsive movements, collapsed on his chair for child, he twists his whole body, in the middle of atrocious sufferings which gnaw his entrails, making scrape his file against the wall of the cube. What evil seizes him all of a sudden? Three times, Michel Fourniret utters piercing cries that have nothing human about them, then stiffens like a log, before bringing his hands to his neck, with the intention of clenching his glottis until he suffocates, all tongue out. Woe! His hands

! How abnormally big they are for a man of his size! God! What disproportion! Ah! to think that the door is stuck!... Get up, Selim! Do something! The ogre, all trembling, is dying, that's for sure! Then, ah! the crisis stops suddenly. In front of our discomfited faces, Michel Fourniret's mouth stretches in a strange rictus. Then, all of a sudden, he laughs so hard he can't hold his ribs. He even wets his handkerchief from his back pocket. So this shaking was just a poorly staged mimicry of the symptoms of advanced Parkinson's disease. Really? What a sad clown! O Fourniret! Where do you find the strength to joke?

Michel Fourniret, *distraught with astonishment* - Parkinson? Me? Oh! Oh! What a crazy idea! If your father, son, was subject to rickets in his early childhood, he had, apart from the flu, not the slightest disease other than a goddamn pride to be smacked around, that's about it. Where did you get that?

Selim. - I got the information from a journalist from France Télévisions. It is clear that he was mistaken.

Michel Fourniret, *going from joy to anger* - Are you referring to this carpet merchant, this bootblack, whom you mentioned in your last letter? This Muraille... is that it? Here! We'll call him that from now on: Crasse-tel. After all, he doesn't deserve much better. This guy lives up to this sobriquet of the carpet class.

Selim, *raising his eyebrows with a surprised look* - Spare me your antics.

Michel Fourniret. - Great spirit is yours! Only great minds have such an innate ability to contradict and even deny themselves. You contacted me one day to tell me exactly: "If this Muraille comes to write to you, know that he is lying about everything. Do not answer him under any circumstances. Phew! Such versatility on your part is rather confusing. Instead of sending him off, turning your back instantly, you had the stupidity, the unconsciousness, the weakness, to listen to his crap. You offered him, by opening yourself, the access to the defects of your armour. Ah! your sensibility of a mistreated toddler... Innocent soul delivered in pasture to the vultures! Blessed bread for such an engeance without faith nor law, nor the least sense of ethics, or respect of others ! Heracles, when he put on the tunic of Nessos, felt such pain when he felt his skin burning under the effect of the poison that he ended his life.

Selim, *impatiently* - I'm free to turn a sordid news story into a pirate adventure.

Michel Fourniret. - Thanks to this kind of washing machine, this mural and other scavengers of journalists - unworthy of a capital letter - would take their toll. Thus, the face of these scavengers would be less shiny, what shall I say? Superbly shabby! Ah! if I had in front of me one of these journalists who came up with this nonsense, there, now... Ah! believe me! He would feel it!

Then, turning to me, he waves his fist under my nose, from a distance.

Me, *distraught with anxiety* - Hm!

Michel Fourniret. - Hey! You, there! Who are you?

I am Oli. - I am Oli, a friend of Selim. I am here to support him in this terrible ordeal, that's all...

Selim, *flying to my rescue* - From what I can see, you've grown a beard. But it doesn't look like you. What happened? You used to make a point of trimming yourself every morning. What made you change your mind? In the years before your arrest, you were always clean-shaven. Now you don't look like yourself. You have something to hide!

Michel Fourniret, *reflecting* - My beard? Not an aesthetic choice. Let's say I let it grow for convenience. I just trim it, from time to time, to redefine its contours in front of the mirror, using a pair of scissors.

Selim, *full of reason* - Do you ever think of the evil you have done? Don't you ever feel sorry for all those families you have destroyed, forever plunged into mourning and tears because of your fault alone? Am I not one of your many victims?

Michel Fourniret. *the little finger on the seam of the pants* - I can't answer you, because I never really asked myself the question.

Selim. - I'm asking you! Unbelievable! You always have to find a way to escape. And by the way, are you happy to see me?

Michel Fourniret, *questioning* - I can't answer you right now. No, frankly I don't know. It evokes a feeling in me, that's for sure. But I can't tell you what it is. The fact is that you are not omnipresent in my thoughts. However, not a day goes by without me thinking about mine. I need to step back, and I need time to analyze all this. This gives me, in any case, something to write about at length! I'll keep you posted.

Me, *shocked* - Please allow me to intrude on the conversation. Your son is standing in front of you now. This is probably the last time you will ever see him, and you dare to ruin the moment. Selim has flown in to see you in this shithole, you! This is a precious moment. You are ruining it!

Michel Fourniret, *offended* - As far as I know, writing is a means of communication like any other.

Me, *with a wry smile* - On par with violence, right? Hats off to you!

Michel Fourniret, *strengthening his voice* - But who are you, in the end? What is the nature of your links with my son Selim?

Me. - Sir, I don't know you. I thought I already told you that my name was Oli, and that I was a friend of Selim. You are free to turn a deaf ear. Would it be too much to ask you to tell him that you missed him? That it would be a coward to ignore him, who incurred precious expenses to come and see you. Plane, cab, restaurants, hotel, and so on... All this cost him a lot of money, and you are not even able to tell him if his coming warms your heart... It is a world! Maybe you think you are in a dressing room where time has no hold?

Michel Fourniret, *running his hand through his pearly hair* - What are you saying?

Me, *pointing to the screened, opaque window* - You see that window. There, just down the street! It's not a stunt. Outside, only ten meters away, is Polenta's inn, La Calèche. Selim and I had dinner there last night. So we're going back there for lunch in about half an hour.

Michel Fourniret, *lost in astonishment* - Oh, so that...

The "ogre of the Ardennes" gets up, and, walking towards the barricaded window, in the little light crossing the bars, his face takes a very strange expression. The brightness deepens his wrinkles, suddenly revealing the contours of an expression of revolted surprise, around his grimacing mouth. What does it mean? the lost eyes, he approaches even more the sanded window, and woe! examines it as if he had just made a prodigious discovery. As you know, his prison file states that he "applies himself to lose his footing with reality". Am I to understand that he had gone so far as to convince himself that the rest of the world, beyond the walls of his prison, had vanished like a dream, all for the sole purpose of making his detention more pleasant? So it is true. He has no conception of reality.

Selim. - You have never held me in your arms. I tell you that I am going to get married, but you, well! you don't care at all.

Michel Fourniret, *lyrically* - As said before, nothing is important. Everything is important. We have time.

Selim. - We don't have time!

Michel Fourniret, *deaf to his complaints* - At any age, until his death, my father, the fitter Jules Louis Gaston Fourniret, born on May 8, 1899 in Moiry, did not care that I had become an adult. Immanently, out of our meetings, and this until the end of his journey here below, he called me by "Ah ! fiston" or "Te v'là, gamin ? More authentic, true, than any lyricism, this modest laconism warms the heart.

Selim. - Is it true what they say about you? You brag about being "bad, devoid of any human feeling". Are you making fun of me? Everyone has feelings. Even today, I remember your reaction when the house phone rang that morning in 1995. You had just been told that your son, Nicolas, had died in a wood chipper. I remember very well how you reacted to the news of his death.

Michel Fourniret, *the nostrils inflated* - That has nothing to do with it. It's irrelevant.

Selim. - You're right, it's worse! You committed crimes, murders! If Nicolas killed himself at work, Marie-Hélène, on the other hand, committed suicide because of you! In the same way, all those little girls were murdered by your own hands. It is you who killed them. For their families, Fourniret is the only cause of their grief. When you were announced the death of Nicolas and Marie-Hélène, you were in the same state as these families that you despise so much, do you realize it? Why? They are people like you. They all had the same reaction as you. Really, you are not ravaged by remorse when you realize the extent of your record? Why don't you confess your other crimes?

Michel Fourniret, *his eyes shining with tears* - Sometimes, I can't stand myself. I think I'm an idiot, an idiot who can slap me around! I am a big idiot! But I assume. I don't regret it. It's all due to my immeasurable, boundless pride.

Selim, *shrugging his shoulders* - There you go again! I warn you, this is the last time you'll see me. If you want to talk to me, it's now or never. For me, you're dead.

Michel Fourniret, *showing a complete bewilderment* - Yes, it is true that "socially", I am dead.

Selim. - Do not pretend you do not understand. I repeat, you are dead in my heart. I am not your son anymore. My parents died in a serious accident. That's what I tell everyone. You said it yourself: "Little Selim is no more. For me, Michel Fourniret and Monique Olivier are just names. Of course, you don't like André Michaut, but he was like a father to me, the only one I ever had... He took me in under his roof, raised me like his own son, fed me, gave me clothes... Nothing obliged him to take under his wing the son of the man who had promised to kill him, but he did it without expecting anything in return. Yes, André was good to me. He behaved like a father, supporting me with his encouragement and his money. This is not the case with your brother, André Fourniret. He said he did not want to shelter under his roof the son of a criminal "who is surely the same". Then Marvin arrived, as if by miracle! Thanks to him, I didn't kill myself, like Marie-Hélène. Do you understand?

Michel Fourniret, *disoriented and tenderized* - Well, it's possible that I was wrong about André Michaut, even if he's just a little driving instructor...

Selim, *vaguely surprised* - It's a need, it's stronger than you! You always need to put others down. Always! But what have you done for me? You keep invoking a father/son relationship. A relationship is based on a mutual exchange, a dialogue... Except that with you, everything is one way. Your letters are aggressive, meaningless, and expect no response. You listen to yourself. You are the one who wanted to get in touch. What do you expect from me? I certainly don't expect anything anymore. Sending me money is the only way you can avoid paying the compensation imposed by the court. A flurry of arms of honor to the families of the victims, to whom you have caused irreparable harm. I'm telling you! I will never again accept a cent from you. Oh, never! If you want to get rid of this money, just send a check to the order of Les Restos du Cœur, along with a completed and printed support form to : Les Restaurants du Cœur - Service donateur - 42, rue de Clichy - 75009 Paris.

Me. - If the press is to be believed, you have a much higher than average IQ. In all honesty, with hindsight, given the turn of events, wouldn't you have preferred to rise in dignity by leading a tidy little life as an engineer, holier and more perfect, away from the little girls who arouse the most vile impulses in you, joining your own at the Sautou estate every evening, rather than making old bones behind bars?

Michel Fourniret, *shaking his head* - I don't care what the press has said about me, whether it's good or bad.

Me. - You know, on television, entire programs are dedicated to you. The ultimate consecration, you will one day be the subject of a film, that's for sure!

Selim, *with a pungent irony* - Outside, you are a real star! A big bravo! Everyone calls you the "Ogre of the Ardennes".

Michel Fourniret, *looking outraged* - Pfff!

Selim, *surreptitiously involving me in his quarrel* - It's not the scribblers' fault that the affair is making the headlines. It is you who gave them grist for the mill. After all, who raped, strangled and killed? They only did their job.

Michel Fourniret. - It's true, you're right.

Selim, *about Esau during the Ranucci trial* - By the way! I attached an old photo of you to my last letter. What did you think of it?

Michel Fourniret. - You're right to mention it, son. In spite of the trained memory that is mine, I have no recollection of any photograph.

The photographic portrait of Esau, has it vanished? Gone! As if by magic! For me, the case is clear. It was deliberately removed from the sight of prisoner 5451. Of course, this sabotage is the work of the censorship committee. Nothing is less certain! Why keep this picture out of Michel Fourniret's reach, suggesting that it is a matter of a defense secret related to his twin condition? They know everything. They know who Esau is. At least, they know that this man photographed in front of the Aix-en-Provence court of assizes in 1976 is none other than Michel Fourniret himself, and that he may have played a role in the murder of Marie-Dolorès Rambla, for which Ranucci was guillotined. Otherwise, why do such a thing at the risk of accrediting our hypothesis? Perhaps this act of censorship is intended to avoid the prospect, however remote, of a resumption of the debates surrounding the "red sweater" affair?

In 2006, the experts were formal. An anthropometric study of Esau's photos showed that he could not be the

"Ogre of the Ardennes". The mass media then declared: "Fourniret was not at the Ranucci trial".

Christian Ranucci from Nice was the first convict to perish on the guillotine during the seven-year term of former French head of state, Valéry Giscard d'Estaing. In 2018 Giscard is still alive, aged ninety-one. Questioned about the case in 2010, the former president had confided that he had no regrets despite the few grey areas, and swore that he would have maintained the death penalty if he had been re-elected in 1981. Still, Selim Fourniret attests today on his honor that the man photographed in 1976 - this Esau - is indeed his father.

Michel Fourniret. - And what did this photo show?

Selim. - You, from your youth, in the 1970s. I found it by chance, while tidying up. The opportunity to make sure that it was really you on it. A simple rhetorical question. I know it's you! I know because - ah, it hurts me to admit it! - it looks like me. I thought you'd like to see it again, but the censors don't agree. Oh, by the way. The said picture was taken near Marseille.

Michel Fourniret. - I know the region well, having been there once as a young man, when I had just been drafted into the French army. I had to embark on a boat to reach the battlefield in Algeria, where I served in the Air Commandos. I was only a conscript, a simple soldier!

Me. - Did you fight in the Algerian war?

Michel Fourniret, *curtly* - Sir, the Algerian war was made by itself! Take it for granted! After a half-century sleep, snatches of martial songs shouted at twenty years old, under the black beret of the 50.541 airborne commando company, resurface. On the road, near an old oak tree, a soldier is there, posted. He is listening. He finds his memories of his past. His village with the fresh shades, where his fiancée awaits him under the freshly bloomed roses. She is waiting for the hoped-for return. On the road, near an old oak, a soldier is there. Fallen. The continuation escapes me, but will return! Half a century? It is only a parenthesis!

Selim, *convinced that this is a cruel reference to Hasna, the Algerian woman from Khenchela -* You're annoying me! Now you're going to tell me why you keep referring to Algeria for some time! No lies! Not this time!

Michel Fourniret, *with an affected look. -* But what are you looking for? I don't understand. It's in vain that I reread the copies of the letters I sent you. I swear to you! There's nothing negative in the memories that I treasure from the eighteen months I spent in the army in Algeria.

Selim. - Let me be allowed to doubt it!

(*A prolonged silence.*)

Michel Fourniret, *rushing towards me, sniffing out the well-tried skulduggery tactic -* For the last time, sir, what have you come here for? Who are you?

I, *with the intention of destabilizing him -* You've already asked me that question three times. So, be frank. What's bothering you so much, sir? Were you afraid that Selim and I might be a homosexual couple, is that it?

Michel Fourniret, *in a softened voice, fooled by the subterfuge -* No, not at all, no, no.

Me, *in a more solemn tone -* Listen, the reason we're here today is so that you can explain to Selim how to deal with the death threats. Maybe you don't know that there is a price on Selim's head...

Michel Fourniret, *he shudders with astonishment -* Hey, what the hell is this?

Me. - Are you unaware that there are people with bad intentions who want Selim's head? He remains a potential target for gangsters, whose honor you have violated, it is no secret. All your crimes could cost him a national vindication. A robber like Jean-Pierre Hellegouarch may very well want to attack him to get to you, and with reason...

Michel Fourniret, - Ah! Hellegouarch... He was really a nice guy with a rare intelligence! One of the nicest people I met in prison... I don't see why he would go after you, Selim...

Selim, *revolted* - Are you kidding me? In 1988, you killed his wife, Farida, with a bayonet. Her body was never found. All to get your hands on the loot you were supposed to share with her. At home, there was money everywhere, ah! that I remember...

I am. - You probably don't know it, but Jean-Claude Myszka des Postiches put an end to his life when he understood that he would never find the gold that you stole from him, the one thanks to which you acquired the Sautou castle.

Michel Fourniret, *his voice full of dismay* - I... I didn't know. Besides, it goes without saying that if André Bellaïche was standing in front of me, in your place, I would have a hard time, that goes without saying...

Me. - Just how much was in that trunk?

Michel Fourniret, *a bit amused, pretending to lift two big weights* - Oh, I would say two good weights!

Me. - That's what allowed you to live the high life in your castle, in the Sautou domain...

Michel Fourniret, *a bit flattered* - Yes, it's true. However, my goal was never to become a squire. Initially, I had to refurbish the Sautou to increase its resale value and make a nice profit.

I did. - That's when the Breton arrived and shot you, after which you fled, leaving Selim and Monique Olivier at the mercy of a seasoned gangster, armed to the teeth... By the way, don't you have any problems with the other inmates? It is commonly believed that in prison, pedophiles are given a hard time...

Michel Fourniret, *out of his mind, showing off his little biceps* - No! Even so, I'd have some, right? I'm not afraid of a fight. At worst, it will make me muscles, in many ways!

Selim. - Do you understand that families are still suffering from not knowing what happened to their children, whom you probably killed? Imagine your reaction, if someone did to me what you did to them... How would you react?

Michel Fourniret, *affected of repentance, without encumbering himself of additional considerations for the small* - Listen, you asked me if I felt regrets with regard to the past, well! there is a thing which I regret bitterly. It is to have killed Farida. I should never have done it, if only out of respect for Jean-Pierre Hellegouarch, whom I like very much... A nice guy, really!

Me. - And what about poor Joanna Parrish? The case is not even closed yet. Besides Farida Hammiche, her death should soon be the subject of a new trial, if I am not mistaken...

On May 17, 1990, a fisherman discovered the lifeless body of twenty-year-old Joanna Parrish in Monéteau, on a bank of the Yonne River. The investigation concluded that the young English assistant had been raped and murdered. An unsolved murder. Twenty-seven years later, her parents asked the French investigators to re-interview the main suspects, including Michel Fourniret. Monique Olivier had explained that Fourniret was in Auxerre at that time, before retracting... Joanna Parrish was going to become a teacher... Joanna had been bound, then raped before being murdered. Roger Parrish and his ex-wife, Pauline Murrell, are not tender towards the justice and the French investigators. The mother thinks they are Clouseau-like investigators, named after the wacky policeman played by Peter Sellers. "I told them and they know very well what I think of them," her mom told the *Daily Mail*. They had arrived in Auxerre three weeks after receiving the tragic news. "When I asked the magistrate who was investigating whether Joanna had been raped, he told me categorically that she had not. He had lied to me, because I learned from the press that it was not true.

A few years ago, a petition was even launched on the Internet by Joanna's brother, who was seventeen years old at the time of the events. He asks that French justice finally answer the question that haunts his parents: "Who killed our daughter? I read in the press that they still hope that a new witness or that the progress of science in DNA analysis will allow, one day, to identify the murderer of Joanna.

Michel Fourniret, *making the formal and precise confession of his crime* - Yes, I have something to do with the death of Joanna Parrish. It is true! But again, I have nothing to do with that of Estelle Mouzin. I have always been straight in my boots! I arrived at the wedding as a virgin, sir! I've never denuded anyone! Since the dawn of time, Mother Nature, never did, never does anything without reason. That never! I can't stand it when someone offends Mother Nature! When the shame that accompanies impotence becomes too hard to bear, one is obliged to suppress the person in front. And then, pow!

(In a sudden, satanic contraction, he mimes, in an indescribable way, breaking the neck of a small imaginary being,

with his hands. His crimes are theorized and assumed. On this subject, Selim will never dare to admit to himself that his father simply sought to liquidate the embarrassing witnesses of the erectile dysfunctions that occurred during his numerous rapes).

Me, *raising my hand to speak* - Another little detail. There is something that bothers me. May I ask you an annoying question?

Michel Fourniret, *honored* - Please do.

Me, *pointing out to her through the translucent glass of the cube the nursery adapted to the little ones* - By chance you evoke Mother Nature, just in front of this pastel colored backdrop on which appears a sacred wood. After all, isn't it offensive to Mother Nature to take the life of her innocent creatures? For, finally, having learned of your history from the media, I know your crimes are full of impiety. Alas!

Michel Fourniret, a *little unsettled* - Oh, that! That's a pertinent question, sir... Pertinent! Until now, I had never seen things from that angle. However, you must understand that it is not the Trinitarian God or nature in itself that we are talking about here.

I am. - The press says that you are - and I quote - "obsessed by the image of the Virgin Mary".

Michel Fourniret, *rubbing his hands together* - It's false, very false! The press tells what suits them. What I'm talking about is the existence of a creative principle proclaimed under the name of Mother Nature. All this will have given me plenty of food for thought for my next letter... I can't wait to get back to my thebaid to put it all down on paper.

Me. - You have to understand that Selim is no longer a child. Today, he works his ass off at five jobs for about 300 hours a month. When you see the responsible adult that Selim has become, do you feel pride in him?

Michel Fourniret, *with that shameless disdain that characterizes him so much* - Proud of Selim? It's all very well to have Tarzan's biscotos, but you still need to have a functional brain to know how to use them wisely. Besides, the job he has to do is small and poorly paid, compared to all the jobs I have done in my life. Selim, you are not an engineer, as far as I know! What the hell! Security guard? Pfff! Look at my hands! I'm proud to be from the Ardennes! These are the hands of workers that you see there! Hey! You, there! Let me see your hands.

(*I hold out my gnarled fingers to him.*)

Michel Fourniret, *staring at them with admiration* - It can go!

Me, *indignant* - The truth is that you don't love your son. You don't give a damn that he suffers! A father worthy of the name would have already apologized...

Michel Fourniret, *tears welling up in his eyes* - What do you dare to say? It goes without saying that there will be a before and after, starting from this day. Don't you understand anything? No two days will be alike. Ah! if someone came to tell me that a volcano has just erupted, 30 meters away, I would answer: I don't give a damn, pov'idiot! You can sit on it. Don't you see that Selim is here? Selim is there. The rest is irrelevant. "Whether volcanoes are extinct or awake is a whole[24].

Me. - Do you understand the reasons for Selim's anger? What! Do you still not know? What happened in your absence is terrifying...

Michel Fourniret. - What are you talking about?

---

24. Sentence taken from The *Little Prince* by Antoine de Saint-Exupéry.

Me. - Selim was fifteen years old when your wife was arrested in Waulsort on June 28, 2004. At the time, the police officers said they had to take her to the station to ask her some questions. But she never came back. At 15 years old, after his mother's arrest, the boy was left alone, without recourse, abandoned for almost a week, completely on his own, in a state of shock. Oh no, you are not dreaming! The Belgian social services did not take care of him. And it lasted a week! It was only a child... But finally, it is not the kind of thing likely to shock you...

Selim. - During that week, I was alone. The few times I went out, it was to walk the dog. Do you remember Flicka? To be honest, I felt so miserable... I thought of killing myself... I owe my life only to my cowardice. Yes, I am a coward. I should have died...

Michel Fourniret. - Sorry, Selim. I didn't know. It's all my fault...

Me. - Do you understand now that he may be angry with you? His tone may seem aggressive at times, but talking helps him release his anxieties.

Michel Fourniret. - Ah ! the catharsis... The ca-thar-sis !

Me. - Beyond that, how do you expect him to live a normal sexuality? After all, you raped, and killed girls old enough to be his friends. Because of you, he can't stop thinking about it when he's around a woman.

(*An embarrassed silence*).

Michel Fourniret, *in a plaintive and dolorous voice* - Once again, I had never seen things in this light. I didn't know. It is so sad...

Selim, *ingenious* - It was you who nailed me to that wood. Everything I went through because of you made me stronger. Few people have experienced what I have endured. I was brought down to the ground, but I got up again. Yes, your crimes have made me stronger. This is the story of a child who lost his parents during the war. His house was destroyed. So he digs for treasure. He searches. It was beautiful, but it was sad. The good times!

(*A heavy silence crushes the cube. The ogre sketches a smile*).

Selim and Michel Fourniret, *reciting a nursery rhyme* with the *same voice, in communion, both driven by a secret instinct, under my stunned eyes* - It was beautiful, but it was sad/ The fire captain was crying in his helmet/ A drop fell on a peach pit that sprouted/ The king's son passed by, fell down, and killed himself/ They gave him a magnificent funeral/ It was beautiful, but it was sad.

Michel Fourniret, *speechless, impressed by the perspicacity of his son* - Oh! So you remember. Unheard of! It was me who taught you that...

Selim. - I also remember this book that you forced me to read: *Les Hauts Murs* by Auguste Le Breton. The story of a betrayed childhood! Yes, remember, the hard story of this fourteen year old orphan who fights to survive in a reformatory, losing little by little his innocence. He revolts in the face of violence, while hoping to quickly find a way to rebuild his life in New York, in the United States. The Breton! What an irony, isn't it?

Michel Fourniret. - Now, ask me anything you want, Selim. I will tell you everything, absolutely everything!

Selim. - I want to know what's left, and where to dig.

Michel Fourniret. - What is it?

Selim, *gritting his teeth horribly* - You know that very well. The treasure of the Postiches! I am listening.

(*A dark premonition.*)

Michel Fourniret. - I... Oh yes! Uh... He... But come on, Selim, there's nothing left, come on! What the hell! What an idea! There is no treasure except in your wild imagination. I exchanged all the gold bars for silver, in Brussels, with a Jew named Hermann.

To my dismay, all is lost. So for two years, I devoted all my energy to developing a totally chimerical narrative arc, which kept me bent. We are played out! What's the point of lying to your son on such a glorious day? I must resign myself. Michel Fourniret is telling the truth. You scum! So the treasure was just a whim. A mirage!

I only see this solution... It's up to you, Selim! Let's not waste any more film on this pedophile lout. Gather all your strength and crush the villain! Give the bastard a kick in the ass!

Selim, *feeling supported by a kick to the ankle* - Excuse me for insisting, but do you remember when you were called to tell you that Nicolas had killed himself? What did you feel? The ground gave way under your feet! The sky fell on your head! You literally broke down! You were inconsolable, even crying! Ho! Ho! What a bad job for a guy of your caliber, self-proclaimed "worse than Dutroux"! Ho! Ho! Ho!

Michel Fourniret, *his glibness suddenly cooled by emotion* - Nicolas ? An accident at work in the Orne region, caught by the drum of a barker. The day before our Christmas reunion, euphoric, distracted, he let his guard down. This? On April 18, 1996. Twenty-four year old Nicolas was the victim of an accident. While he was distracted, his scarf got stuck in the shredder. My God... Nicolas... Nicolas...

Selim, *with a mischievous, insolent look* - You may present yourself as an individual with a superior intelligence quotient, but you are still a poor fellow who needs to be demystified, and whose coffin only needs to be shaved. You say in a weeping tone that Marie-Hélène committed suicide because of the "media effervescence" of the Fourniret affair, implying that it would be the fault of journalists. You know better than me that this is not true. Great coward! You killed her, Michel. The poor girl died of shame!

It's a success! In the bull's eye! Without caring about my gaze fixed on him, the "ogre of the Ardennes" bursts into tears, without any restraint. Hot tears are escaping from his bluish eyelids. He swallows his tongue. The song of the swan! Reduced to pieces, the head inclined on the chest, he starts again to push big funeral cries, doubled by alas, sheathing his tremolos. To finish, he pushes a tyrolienne in prey to a crazy terror. " Nicolas! Ni-co-las! Ni-co-las! Ni-co-las!", he neighs to give up the soul.

Selim. - Now stop braying like a donkey! If you are not happy, you should have stayed where you were, in your thebaid. A father who hasn't seen his son for a decade should be happy to hear from him, ask him questions, even beg forgiveness for his sins... How are you? What do you do for a living? What is your fiancée's name? How did you meet? Ha! Ha! Ha! This would be a great misunderstanding of Michel Fourniret who, in all cases, remains distant. However, I am alive and well. Unfortunately, I know your fascination for death. In the end, it took Nicolas losing his life for you to finally consider him as your son. He died trying to be like his father, working with his hands so that you would recognize his efforts, his values... Something that finally happened when you announced his death. A little late, isn't it? A few years later, it was Marie-Hélène's turn to lie in a nameless grave. Once again, it was only at this point that you had any consideration for her... A little late, no?

Hell is repetition. So what? What should I do, if not die? What must Selim do to be recognized by you? Should I go and join Nicolas in the afterlife? Here is a new question that you will hasten to evade - I know it - by a declamatory text.

***

"Click! Clack!" Here comes some backup. Someone is coming to the door. The latch moves, agitates. "Hey, there! It's a real mess here! Who dares to interrupt our work? "Whoa, Oli! Go and see who is knocking like that...", says Selim. At the edge of the door, the jailer, surely alerted by the strange commotion that agitates the glass cube, similar to an opium den. With panicked gestures, he tries to open the door, but finds that it is barricaded with an unspeakable spell. He then gives a blow in the door with the point of his boot. "Hey, the door is taken!" I shouted, excitedly. "Open us... The best thing is to break the door down!" With a violent push, I hesitate to rush at Michel Fourniret to unload a volley of furious blows in the solar plexus, in the name of all the parents of the lost children, and who would dream - I know it - to be in my place in this moment. On guard! The fist clenched in a ball, I search in me the heroic immemorial bravery inherited from the forefathers beyond the strait of Messina, between Charybdis and Scylla, in vain. What do you want? I cannot, without inhumanity, attack a frail old man with dislocated shoulders. But then, what is my use in this sinister affair? At these cries of agony, the guard waved his set of interlocking keys, gave three turns, opened the door all flapping, and in a loud voice: "It's over." This blow put an end to the ordeal. The dislodged spine, he returns in his thebaid. Then, gradually taking again its natural form, this one tries, all trembling, to flee by the backstage by trying to borrow the luminous portal which must bring us back in the real world. The guard calls him to order!

"Our clay paths separate here," I said to Michel Fourniret, with an air of pity. In the long corridor, in front of Selim, the "ogre of the Ardennes", beaten to a pulp, goes away roaring, all clopin-clopin, his back bent under the anathema. "Hey, wait!" Turning to the damned prince of Sautou, who is safe, I ask, frightened, with cloudy eyes: "This is the last time you will see him. Aren't you going to say goodbye to that scoliotic crab?" Selim, seeing his pitiful father so slumped that he could fall, remains for a moment motionless. And, going away, with a distracted and bitter air, he ends up releasing a final imprecation of a strong voice, calling on his father the anger of the infernal divinities:

"May he die!"

Slowly, slowly, he sighs, and goes out. Well, out then! Out! As the doors of the penitentiary close, an as yet unreported discovery whips across my neck, startling me, like a final regret. "Shit! My belt? Where did I put it? I can't see it anywhere! Selim! Didn't you see my wide brown buffalo leather belt?

- Your belt? Look in your bag...

- But no! It's not there... Look!"

While I am about to turn back in haste, the prince of Sautou - in an evidently oedipal mood, as one can think - seizes my arm, almost by force, his eyes round like freshly minted 2 euro coins. There, he declares to me with a lot of accuracy and intelligence, but the articulation is difficult: "For me the matter is clear. It is an expiatory sacrifice in favor of destiny. Your belt? Let him hang himself with it,

20. La Maison-Dieu

this old fool! That's all I ask. That's my opinion," he added, leading me up the stairs. And it is also what I think, dear friend. Melancholic, the loose pants falling on my hips however bulbous, it returns to me in memory this sentence in apparently anodyne, that I repeat to myself several times, the spirit in swing:

"Without laces, nor suspenders, rid of everything that ties and holds me back, I learn to live again. I enter into existence."

21.

A FATHER AT SEA

"Let's try to be happy,
if only to set an example."
Jacques Prévert

Nine months have passed, the time of a birth. The "ogre of the Ardennes" received terrible news. His son Selim is at death's door after a suicide attempt. This hoax hides, in truth, his resurrection, for he is leaving. Yes, he has finally decided to leave. Even before the opening of a new trial that could rekindle stupid desires for revenge, he's leaving to rebuild his life in another part of the world, in a secret corner of the map, where no one - except for him - has ever heard the name Fourniret. Only then will he be able to reinvent his genealogy as he pleases.

During the nine months following our trip to Ensisheim, Selim did not give any sign of life to the belligerent ogre. Not a word. Not a word. It was agreed between us that his eternal silence would be a much harsher sentence than life imprisonment. Never will this villain be given a worse punishment than absolute indifference, applicable from the moment Selim turned his back on him, even as he returned to his murderess, swimming in his tears, in Ensisheim. Unfortunately, the "ogre of the Ardennes", knowing only too well how to infallibly lure Selim into his nets, sent him, on January 28, a remittance of 800 euros "as a contribution to the transportation costs of a person coming from the Alpes-Maritimes to Alsace. An amount of participation in the disbursements caused".

But to continue to accept this money would have been contrary to the original promise never to serve this scumbag soup again. So I urged Selim not to accept anything from him again. This must be perfectly understood, otherwise the story I told you would have no moral value.

Besides, I had to take care of finishing off the odious character by means of a solid test. I knew his weak point, his Achilles heel: Selim. No one else had the power to ignite the spark that would set this dried-up fetus ablaze. Michel Fourniret had to suffer. To get what I wanted, all I had to do was squeeze him like a sponge, and watch, impassive, as his juices slowly poured out in a torrent of dripping pathos, all the while thinking of the souls of the deceased children. May their blood not have been shed without vengeance!

As a response to the act of censorship of the moral authorities - always on the lookout for the slightest detail that could damage the continuity of their interests - I had a lot to do. Everything has been rethought.

During March 2016, I finally managed to get a mosaic of six photographs of Esau, Michel Fourniret's supposed look-alike, into prison, to which I took the liberty of making a few alterations to the form. This is how he ended up with a toothbrush moustache, Hitler style, topped with a bloody swastika on his forehead, an arrow in his skull, as well as a pair of twisted horns and a forked tail, the prerogative of the cuckold. To this, I added a vivid purple coloring of his cheeks, and covered his lips with a garish red, symbol of a putassive vulgarity. Unless to employ these artifices, it would have been impossible to thwart the censorship.

So for the very first time, on April 8, 2016, I took up my pen to write to Michel Fourniret in my name alone. From then on, we were no longer strangers to each other. We made Michel Fourniret believe that Selim was sailing between life and death because of his fault, after having been repeatedly threatened with death by the Postiches gang, who would not hesitate to deliver the coup de grace if his loot was not returned to him.

Me, *to Michel Fourniret* - What I have to tell you is of the utmost importance. What have I done? Our trip to Ensisheim was supposed to save Selim. Instead, it caused a terrible accident. I feel terrible, because I was the one who convinced him to come to you to deal with his problems, but you disowned him. Mr. Fourniret, you will have understood, I come to you with very sad news. A week ago, Selim tried to end his life by ingesting a large quantity of drugs, before getting on his motorcycle and running away at 200 km/h. Suicide! It is once passed the Italian border that he would have lost the control of his motorcycle, and struck a pylon of freeway. From now on, Selim is plunged in the coma. He was admitted to the emergency room in the province of Imperia in Liguria, on the French-Italian border. I don't know if he will ever wake up. Doctors and surgeons are hopeful that he will recover, but there is a catch... This type of accident is likely to happen again.

Mr. Fourniret, I have to tell you something else. At the end of February, at the exit of a bar in Cannes, Selim was beaten up by helmeted, leather-clad individuals. The poor guy got one of these beatings! He was found lying in a large pool of blood. There were at least seven of them, he told me. As a result, his jaw had been broken, and he had even had to have four titanium plates put on, after one of the kings had kicked him in the face. Poor Selim! So much suffering... Brutes! Vile scoundrels! Cowards! I can't imagine what it must have been like... For the time being, we still don't know who ordered this punitive mission, but they said they wanted to make Selim pay for being "the son of the pedophile Fourniret". Apparently, they knew about our visit to Ensisheim... A relative of your victims? The last of the Postiches? No one knows.

What is certain, however, is that this event has a link with the gangsters, whose honor you have violated. Selim told me that he feared for his life, without explaining the ins and outs. The reason why he did not tell me about this aggression is surely the fear of reprisals. I did everything I could to protect him from gossip, from this world that condemns everything... If only I had been there that night... This tragedy occurred just as he had offered to volunteer for a bone marrow donation. How unfair life is.

No, no, it's all your fault, I'm a witness. What's the use of crying? In prison, when he visited you, Selim asked you what to do if one of them came to ask him about the treasure. To this, you were unable to answer anything. You are so pathetic. It's already enough to belong to the Olivier/Fourniret pedophile line, if Selim has to pay back your loans, it's the end! Alas! Three times alas! Better to die, indeed...

For the time being, I don't know if the heir of your evils will ever wake up, and perhaps it's better that way, because if one of them came back to the charge, what would he have to answer? Nothing. My God! What have you done? What have you done, Fourniret? You have condemned your own son to suffer the consequences of your crimes. What have you done? Please, do something! Do something! Give me the grace and charity to give these pirates what they want!

***

For a father, I imagine there is no greater and more bitter pain than a dying son. Unbelievable! By an inevitable fate, on April 14, 2016, Selim and his half-brothers, Wendel and Marvin, were auditioned at the Antibes anticriminality brigade within the framework of a rogatory commission issued by the investigating judge in charge of the investigation into the murder of Farida Hammiche. Here again, and in a very curious way, their objective was to draw up - I quote - "a psychological portrait of the Olivier/Fourniret couple". The investigators are still stuck at the stage of profiling, supposedly revolutionary. It is pathetic! Besides, would you believe me if I told you that the hearings of the Olivier siblings took place at the Antibes anticriminality brigade, at 5 Avenue des *Frères-Olivier*"? What an extraordinary coincidence, isn't it?

Finally, the investigators raised the hypothesis of a transfer of Monique Olivier to the women's section of the Nice prison, thinking to push her to confess by this favor. If you are reading me, peacekeepers, you should know that Michel Fourniret confessed, not without a certain amount of bluster, that he eliminated Farida Hammiche, which he bitterly regrets, but also that he had "something to do" with the disappearance of Joanna Parrish. There are also reasons to believe that Michel Fourniret is involved, in one way or another, in the murder of Marie-Dolorès Rambla.

On April 20, 2016, Michel Fourniret - not fooled by my nonsense - answered me this: "Hardly compatible are a matrimonial project and the decision to end one's life. It is not without emotion that I measure the degree of friendship that binds you and Selim. I hadn't thought about it, and it seems to me a valid reason to doubt the veracity of my assertions. Indeed, why would Selim have wanted to kill himself at a time when he should be quietly devoting himself to the preparations for his wedding?

I then found an authentic photo showing Selim in bed, in a plastered corset with neck brace, kept lying down with an IV of antibiotics, which suggests that he was about to give up the ghost. The truth is that this picture was taken in July 2010, when he was in a coma after his motorcycle accident and supposed stroke. To support my lies, I then wrote a short text on the back of the photo. I then had the idea to make him believe that Selim was, like him, obsessed by the question of virginity. By this, I intended to increase the process of identification in a step of setting in confidence to better manipulate him.

So please find attached the content of the text written on the back of Selim's postdated photo, sent to Ensisheim on April 25, 2016:

I, *to Michel Fourniret* - Here is the completion of your work. Here is where your legacy has led your innocent son Selim. You, who are so proud, perhaps you could put your signature at the bottom of this photograph - your work - so that it can be displayed in the Museum of Horrors.

Concerning Selim's marriage project, you should know that it was abandoned when he discovered that his bride was no longer a virgin, that she was cheating on him, and that he only expected to obtain French nationality. All this was a huge source of disappointment for him. He obviously did not see fit to tell you about it. What pride can you take in a gray marriage? Selim wanted so much for you to be proud of him. It's a failure!

P.-S. : Please, Mr. censor, have the decency not to make disappear this photo of Selim, bedridden and sick. Fourniret must see it. Such is the will of his son Selim.

***

Two days later, the administration of the central prison in Ensisheim went out of their way to contact me by phone. No doubt they wanted to know if what I had written was the truth or not. I refused the invitation.

By the way, my plan worked. Thanks to the said six-year-old photograph, Fourniret bought the lie, which deeply disturbed him. From that point on, he began to flail about in desolate terms, to the point of showing human feelings about his "son.

Michel Fourniret, *to Selim* - Screwing up, son? As soon as the cup is too full, not a single drop left. Are we bipeds going through hell? I've got better things to do than offer an accident, plus a nice, cushy coffin. Turn on an engine? Riding a two-wheeler with my nose in the handlebars?

Moved by some wrath? Nicolas, Marie-Hélène ? Your late brothers and sisters, both of them made the beautiful.

Nicolas ? An accident at work in the Orne region, caught by the drum of a barker on December 29, 1995. The day before the reunion, euphoric, distracted, he let his guard down. This? A nameless happiness. Not the time to yawn! Marie? The unmistakable effect of a barbiturate ingestion of a not very chic twin! For the moment, what's done is done. Good reason to piaffe.

What's done is done. Let's not be impatient. Fissa! Convalescence! Fissa! The arm wrestling between Selim Gwenhael Jean-Pierre, and his old Ardennes father. Him? Less inclined to say "I love you" than to utter anathema, fists clenched and sleeves rolled up.

Of course! Olivier, your friend? The real friend! So son, you hang in there! You hang on! You hang on! Do you understand? Anyway, it's not with the road that you have to cross swords, without any foil, but with me, your father! Do you understand? So, go ! Hang in there, son! Life is a marathon. It's not time to kick the bucket! Not without reason, I'm sending you this mercurial, very sharp rant via Olivier. What about him? Nothing of a babi-babot (false-ass in patois of my dear Ardenne). A rare pearl, a good guy! Beware of your chest, son. The father's embrace? Not really that of a soft rag.

This word barely completed on this Monday, May 2, 2016, arrives before my eyes the photograph of Selim in bed, and your lie addressed to the "censor". You write Olivier: "He wanted you to be proud of him. It's failed!" How dare you believe that, Olivier, when I have every reason to be proud of a boy, a son who, knowing what he wants, knew, knows and will always know what he does not want. At no price. The absolute, and the small change, the adulterated, the impure? Incompatible! Our reunion couldn't be worse...

***

Michel Fourniret, *to Selim* - Putting an engine in motion? Riding a two-wheeler... You don't need to be a fox. Proof of this: some cops are motorcyclists. The nose in the handlebars? Driven by some wrath? Terrorizing the users of the highway? Make them tap their temples. "Crazy biker, no doubt!" Belch: what the hell is this guy doing? Probably on fire, this white boy. Dumped by his girlfriend? Thinks he's in a movie? Don Quixote ? Knight with the sad face, riding Rossinante, did not lead great pace thinking :

If I were to break my nose, would I have plastic surgery? Sewn all over, such a pathetic convict? Splash! My sublime project to lead Dulcinea in front of the mayors with scarf and priest in cassock? Also wise to lead my brave motor-cycle. Otherwise? Goodbye to my great projects, my beautiful resolutions! No more, to be for all, the object of admiration. Rubicon alone, once, was crossed by Caesar. At least, thanks to Selim, my Bayard knight: will come in single file, to make amends the minus which dared to jump on the saddle.

So, history repeats itself Olivier, when I read you. Selim's disgusted, disgusted, disgusted, to vomit, to puke, when he learns that his Promise had already a lot of flight hours. When it is already a thousand times too much than flights of a few minutes counted on the fingers of one hand. Indeed, not a little proud to offer himself brand new, back from the army, after eighteen months of epistolary relationship

Algiers-Sedan, the old Selim, to his question: "You're going to have a boo-boo?

The answer "I've already gone to sleep" earned him "sawed-off paws" forever. Daily epistolary relationship. Those who used Annette Lucienne as they pleased, in turn, must have laughed. S.O.S, Selim! S.O.S, Olivier! Help me! A father in the sea!

***

As the days passed, his pain became more acute as our silence became oppressive. So on May 13, 2016, the ogre wrote a shorter, more concise note. This time, he threw himself at Selim's feet to implore him to survive. "Hurry up and get well, kid. It's not from the depths of a hospital bed that you'll be giving your father the finger."

And finally, it happened. The portrait of Esau at the Ranucci trial landed right in the hands of Michel Fourniret, who in turn sent it back to me, offended at having been compared to Hitler, him and not Esau. Do you understand? When Michel Fourniret saw these photos, he was totally confused with his look-alike.

The following letter was written on May 11, 2016, in Alsace. The elements that emerge from it are more than enough to cast doubt on the official version according to which Christian Ranucci was the sole instigator of the murder of Marie-Dolorès Rambla. Was there a Michel Fourniret look-alike on the day of the trial, or was it simply him? Answer of the interested.

Michel Fourniret, *to me, about the mosaic* - Please find, enclosed, in return, an artistic work of first plan, and of which it would be a pity to dispossess the immensely inspired artist that is its author. It would be necessary, at least, that to reach it is possible to an old chnoque carrying a swastika on the forehead, an arrow planted in the skull, and provided with a pair of horns to make any faun green with envy.

***

Look at what I also discovered in another plea, dated June 29, 2016:

Michel Fourniret, *to me* - Your legitimate curiosity, Olivier, would remain on its hunger, a hunger increased by skepticism, if I did not entrust you - for your information as a reader legitimately founded, by wisdom and measure, to skepticism, at the risk of seeing you keep this literary jewel - the document received from my son Selim. Certainly, only four photos out of six decorate "my face". But what: to push me to cut the bridges? One would have been more than enough. Take care of yourself.

***

Michel Fourniret wrote "my face", which forces us to believe that Esau and him are one and the same person. The possessive adjective "my" leaves no possible doubt. Two months later, I received a letter dated July 5, 2016, expressing in a more formal way that Fourniret is indeed the man in the black and white photo:

Michel Fourniret, *to me* - The fact that Selim was able to write a power of attorney for you with his bedridden young hand... What a relief! What a relief! What a desire to open both my windows to thunder, radiant, euphoric, relieved: "That's it, Lady with the scythe, get out! You're no match for my son. Beat it! Faster than that! Shoo! And don't come back!"

Destination, by my apple wished, of this photo where the skull of mézigue saw itself endowed with singular antennas and other attributes which, in its time, made say to Rimbaud Arthur - another Ardennais - among other sublime beauties of his master work *The Drunken Boat*: "Of the shouting Redskins had taken them for targets./ Having nailed them naked to the posts of colors [...] O that my keel bursts! O may I go to the sea!"

Selim's hostile outburst? Effect of legitimate defense mechanisms of a kid who, fatherless and motherless, will be, for the media, the punching bag of the moment. Well! The destination of this photo? Whatever your heart, your head, your guts decide. My only wish is that it goes up in smoke, scattered ashes, and that the place thus freed welcomes this usual thought of Mr. Maxim Gorki: "Often this honey was impure and bitter, but what does it matter, all knowledge is a precious booty."

P.S.: Indiscreet question. Too bad, Mr. Oli Porri Santoro. Are you left-handed from birth? So, really left-handed? Since Mother Nature has never done anything, nor will she do anything, without an excellent reason known only to her, I can't help but think that she wants to make you a fellow who is worth knowing.

✳✳✳

Until now, there has been no document that confirms, in all seriousness, any certainty of Michel Fourniret's involvement in the Ranucci case. No Esau here, it was just Fourniret, from the beginning. This time, all bets are off, because the dictionary definition of the word "mézigue" simply means "me". Fourniret attended the Ranucci trial. There is no doubt about it. "Me".

If Michel Fourniret says so, how can we doubt it any longer? So this is the third coffin that opens here. Do you believe me now? Did Fourniret say "my face", "my apple", and "the skull of mezigue" at the sight of Esau? The answer is yes, three times yes! Esau and Michel Fourniret are - as expected - one and the same. I would not hesitate to rename this one the "Ardennes ogre of the Etang de Berre".

Of course, these are not, strictly speaking, complete confessions by Michel Fourniret, but the simple fact that he can be confused with the beardless Esau can only establish a family link. It is enough! From whatever side you look at the Fourniret case, no one will be able to resist the evidence of this fact.

Recall in your memory the last words pronounced by Christian Ranucci, immortalized in a letter, shortly before his ascent to the scaffold, in 1976, to his mother: "The main thing is that I have my conscience left for me, and that you know that you have nothing to be ashamed of your son, because he has nothing to be ashamed of. Tell all those who have written that they are right to trust me, that I am innocent. One day the truth will come out. Then they will understand what I have endured. I think of you. Loving kiss. Your son Christian."

***

You thought he was dead, but he was preparing his revenge. From there to say that the ogre of the Ardennes was the tiny cog in an immense "special" machine in the disappearance of Marie-Dolorès Rambla, there is only one step that I take without hesitation. For this reason, I officially call for a new discussion of the Esau theory, of which Michel Fourniret is the most perfect symmetry, if only out of respect for the victims' families.

The Belgians were the first to put forward the Esau hypothesis, after which Nachbar and his colleagues ridiculed them. While preparing this investigation, and while reading carefully, I discovered the stifled appeals of the families of the victims, who only received mortifying contempt for the fruit of their beautiful utopias. Moreover, I do not forget that another ghost haunts the Opera, hidden behind three large columns. Remains, indeed, this mysterious P.P.D.

Now, there is nothing more to prevent me from calling upon the vigilantes of infamy, and upon all their families, the vengeance of the screaming ghosts of the little girls who, if they could resurrect on purpose, would stretch out their frail broken wrists and implore: "What have you done, you, with our honor, with our death? But, those will say to me, who is this commoner puffed up with pride who holds us up, and who dares to impose his revolutionary truths on us? A martyr, certainly!

If you want to know, I'll tell you. I am that vague glimmer in the eye of my celestial grandfather Francesco "*Cicciù*" Santoro, when on July 11, 1971, with good looks and affable mood, he became Francis.

Now everything is just and perfect. Since it is so, let's leave, let's leave, yes, but with a bang! Let's get it over with!

In the light of these elements, I embroidered a last bulletin board on which I traced three letters: D.C.D.

This time, it was a question of telling the whole truth, the one that hurts. To do this, there was no need to imagine a text. I let myself go in the most honest way possible. In order to affirm my rank as an embedded journalist, I had a black and white version of my first interview with Selim printed, which appeared in February 2014 in *VSD*, which, for the record, was entitled "For me, my parents are dead," something the ogre had never yet read. This document bore as a preamble the silhouette of Selim in medallion, affixed by my care with a long nose of cleft very similar to that of Pinocchio, suspended above the Mediterranean Sea.

Me, *to Mr. Fourniret -* The truth is, I don't have any respect for you. I even have the worst opinion of you. These last three years, did you really think you were corresponding with Selim? Pinocchio versus Geppetto? Well, no! It has always been me. Me, the journalist for whom you had admiration. You're just a fool. And I thought you hated journalists! Not once did you understand that it was me, me, and nobody else. I'm a ventriloquist, you see. Shame! Ah, I've got you now, you infamous child molester! Even your son disowned you. The long-awaited fight between Pinocchio and Geppetto has finally taken place. Nobody respects a child killer. It's not because you are impotent, and Monique is unbeatable, that you should have attacked innocent little girls. A treasure? What treasure? Besides, may this sentence of Saint Peter, in the Acts of the Apostles, convince you to abdicate: "May your money perish with you, because you thought to acquire the gift of God with money."

You're just a madman trapped between four walls, four planks, and who applies himself to "lose his footing with reality", out of cowardice. It plays with knives, it rapes and strangles little girls, then it whines like a girl! 0/20.

Marie-Angèle Domece, Isabelle Laville, Fabienne Leroy, Jeanne-Marie Desramault, Élisabeth Brichet, Natacha Danais, Céline Saison, Manaya Thumpong, Farida Hammiche, Joanna Parrish, Marie-Dolorès Rambla, and so many others to whom you have subjected to a thousand tortures? Indeed! Here you are, worthy of wearing the dunce's cap that is due to you forever. Splash! You were wrong to attack them, Fourniret! Very wrong! You've just been knocked out by a lefty. Hit and run, and tarred and feathered. The game is over. In prison for eternity, that's where you belong. Surely, I won't waste my time evangelizing a redneck like you. May you perish. No more laughter. The ghosts of the little girls are screaming for death, demanding their fill of Fourniret.

Woe to thee! May the plague burst your belly, and draw omens from your entrails! Fourniret, you're an odious man. Go and hang yourself! Hail! Hallelujah! Hallelujah! Sing the sacrificial lamb! With my best memory. Greet the charming soap.

***

To conclude this chapter in beauty, I lengthened a whip with the pedophile, by condemning him urgently to the gallows by scribbling, in margin, a good man match with beard and binoculars, hoisted high on the ladder of a gallows forming a square, in reversed "L", and wriggling at the end of a cord, in accordance with the game of the hangman.

Inside a bubble, I made Fourniret say this, in the middle of a torrent of tears: "Ni-co-las! Ouch, ouch, ouch! Ni-co-las!" Dirty vermin, take this!

In addition, as a postscript, I added: "That's it! The string is strong, the stone is heavy, there is nothing left to do but to throw the whole thing." This is precisely what a policeman says in *Tintin in the Land of the Soviets*, while he plans to drown Snowy at the bottom of a pond, yes a pond... And now, dance, Fourniret! It's your turn! Come on, dance! Here is his reaction:

Michel Fourniret, *to Selim and me -* This? Although I see *red* and am in a *rage,* this is not the time to come to me. Free to your common bullshit to join the circus. I am not a Santoro who can play Zorro. My failing ears (misdeeds of the work in noisy industry - in particular in workshops of tools of hot stamping), did not allow me to hear your answer to my question: "Your job, it is what?

I thought I heard "manipulator".

Epilogue

So this is the last time Selim and I will drink together. Seated at the sunny terrace of a café in the *blue diadem*, the son of the ogre raises his chalice-shaped glass, collects himself for a moment, then resolves to drink it all. On the point of being released from any attachment, he plunges his glance in the bottom of the container, decorated with the mentions "Duralex" and "3", swimming in heady effluences, and exclaims, blessed:

"I'm three years old.

Happy age! And you will grow up again!"

At the pier of the Nice-Côte d'Azur airport, I say a last goodbye to Selim who, with his impassivity, remains on his own, as always. We don't have time to shed a tear. Go on then! Without dragging, he answers me with a nod of the head, then walks with a sure step towards his goal, dragging behind him an empty suitcase. Go, pilgrim, continue your quest. "Go your way, let nothing stop you. Forget the ephemeral.

Happy, it dissolves in the crowd and in the noise, free of any domination. Leaning against the rail, I put my right hand under my throat to contain the boiling of passions that are already stirring in my chest. When the time comes, a plane, scorched by the light, rises on the middle of the water, above the sharp waves, where a high column of white clouds rises, and then it evaporates. The sky is empty. And so Selim, peace and blessings upon him, goes to the New World, safe from all kinds of evil. Never again will he hear of Michel "*Esau*" Fourniret.

If I did all this, it was for adventure. To get out of the henhouse I bought on credit to fight the soporific routine in which men get stuck. I wanted to escape boredom. Even if I failed, I like to think, like Dubuffet, that "life is a party much more interesting than the pseudo parties that we institute to make people forget it".

With Selim, we saw through the bars of our prison. We braved a thousand perils - useless, of course - but very real. To rise to the size of the "ogre of the Ardennes" was no easy task, but we succeeded. Together, we worked tirelessly to improve ourselves. We accustomed our minds to conceive only ideas of honor and virtue. Three years during which my heart turned to piracy, and I lived with the possibility that we might one day dig up the King's tape. It's still upsetting, in the end, to be mocked by a pedophile... Whatever! O Fourniret, may you be hanged, high and short, and by the beard, in the public square! The promise is an act. "To say is to do.

The following June 24, I receive a message from a foreign number inviting me to click on a link to see a video. On the stoop of my building, I lean against a wall, my posture very low to avoid the glare. I start reading. Under a shower of golden sand, in the middle of birds, we guess a biker in a lunar suit. He flies over a cloud of dust on the burning asphalt. On all sides, golden reflections. He weaves his way between the colourful tanks on a boundless road, lined with cactus, hurtling towards the horizon. Here is again the prince of Sautou ! Splendid! Wonderful! What a joy to see you again, the well furnished purse, out of the Spaggiari tunnel! Happy the great wounded of the soul who can express himself, peremptorily, at the end of a long journey to the paces of wandering, paraphrasing Baudelaire: "You gave me your mud, and I made gold of it." May you finally be free! At least there, they won't come looking for you.

For my part, all day long, I would have done no better than the valiant knight Walter Raleigh who, in 1595, was charged by Queen Elizabeth I of England to go in search of El Dorado, thus leading him to explore - in vain - Guyana. Whatever my intentions were, I return from my vain odyssey without money, nor even provisions...

Did some details wrongly considered null and void escape my attention? Yes, probably! Who knows, maybe I didn't push the analysis far enough. The treasure of the Postiches gang will remain for me an inexhaustible subject of interrogation, so that I will not cease to turn over the problem in my mind scattered in a sterile abundance of paperworks. In the times to come, overannuated and puny, it is not excluded that a flash of genius crosses my meninges, making me stand up with a start in a bed of alumina straw. In the case of memory, I will then understand that all this gibberish was not only Gallic, concert of autolouanges and other traps of the ego, but well a differential equation.

Sometimes I look for one thing and find another. It only remains for me to make against fortune good heart. In my misfortune, I found nothing worthy of grace, nothing except a few coquettish frills: a nice collection of "Femen" stamps, a "toothbrush for loudmouths" (B.A.D.P.G.G.)

and, as a bonus, an information sheet duly accommodated in Syldavian style.

That's it, that's all I could do. And now, to cover the strident "Oh!" of the ogre who horns me in the ears, I sometimes draw from its sheath the chromatic harmonica formerly offered, very generously, by the Holy Virgin, and make resound highly in his honor this tune, which pierces my heart:

***

If by any chance you feel like playing pirate, I have here a map of Waulsort marked with a cross, which you will find on the next page. It contains precise indications on the place where the prince of Sautou had dug the gold tomb with Monique Olivier, thirteen years ago now. This map is not the one found at Selim's, but an exact copy, nicely drawn and complete in every respect. It was entirely redesigned by a friend from the notes and drafts left by the Prince du Sautou who, before his departure, took care to explain everything to me in detail.

If you feel like dredging the Meuse, there's really no harm in taking up my torch at an ungodly hour, equipped with a Galileo scope and a metal detector. Here and there you will comb the forest of shadows, where gold may still be sleeping. A time machine would have been more useful, I agree... If so, it's right here that you'll find a telluric scar in a criss-cross pattern, chattering between two or three shards of polished stone, covered with wood and thorns. As an advice, I will content myself with telling you that whoever wants to give a ploughing must work in winter, because "when the ground is spongy, one digs better..."

I forgot a detail. I can't resist the pleasure of quoting it... Before you go into the mountainous King's Wood in the footsteps of the Prince of Sautou, under the canopy of the great gold trees that filter the light, please remember this proud motto learned from the very respectable Walt Disney, and which will be - I hope forever - my epitaph, traced with soap on a black marble :

"There is certainly more wealth in one book than in all the loot brought back by the pirates of *Treasure Island.*"

Acknowledgements

My thanks go first of all to the illustrator Fanny Rey who put up with my exaltation and my declining mood during the elaboration of this book for years, and who nevertheless agreed to design the illustrations for the *Son of the Ogre*, including the magnificent and authentic treasure map.

I thank my mother Nunziata Carla and my grandmother Giuseppa. A special thanks to Roger-Louis Bianchini, the greatest specialist in organized crime issues, who convinced me to write this book, sharing the ardent enthusiasm that the dark areas of the Fourniret case inspired in me. Thanks to him for his advice and his precious friendship.

My gratitude also goes to Laurence Pieau of the Mondadori group, who allowed me to hold the pen with the other hand, on the rare occasions when I got my head above water.

It is impossible for me to close this book without thanking Jean-Claude Elfassi, without whom this book would never have been published.

I can't thank them enough.

Table of contents

Dedication 9

1. Awakening 13
2. Selim 27
3. The ogre appears.. 35
4. The Prince without a Kingdom 39
5. The line of the palm tree............................. 51
6. The supplicant of the Atlas 57
7. Long John Fourniret.................................. 65
8. A miracle happens 73
9. Prometheus in chains 89
10. Andre the Magus...................................... 99
11. Valentine's Day Massacre............................ 115
12. Special machines 123
13. Whiplash... 133
14. Casus Belli... 141
15. In the lion's mouth 149
16. Crime of apostasy.................................... 155
17. Gold fever 165

18. Selim the freedman 177

19. Good resolutions 195

20. La Maison-Dieu 205

21. A father at sea... 255

Epilogue 273

Acknowledgements....................................... 279

BEST SELLERS MAX MILO EDITIONS

Hitler's banker, Jean-François Bouchard

Confessions of a forger, Éric Piedoie Le Tiec

The Koran and the flesh, Ludovic-Mohamed Zahed

Governing by fake news, Jacques Baud

Governing by chaos, Collectif

A political history of food, Paul Ariès

Mad in U.S.A.: The ravages of the "American model",
Michel Desmurget

Mondial soccer club geopolitics, Kévin Veyssière

Putin: Game master?, Jacques Braud

Treatise on the three impostors: Moses, Jesus, Muhammad,
The Spirit of Spinoza

TV Lobotomy, Michel Desmurget